OCS Study
MMS 2002-077

Coastal Marine Institute

Offshore Petroleum Platforms: Functional Significance for Larval Fish Across Longitudinal and Latitudinal Gradients

U.S. Department of the Interior
Minerals Management Service
Gulf of Mexico OCS Region

Cooperative Agreement
Coastal Marine Institute
Louisiana State University

OCS Study
MMS 2002-077

Coastal Marine Institute

Offshore Petroleum Platforms: Functional Significance for Larval Fish Across Longitudinal and Latitudinal Gradients

Authors

Richard F. Shaw
David C. Lindquist
Mark C. Benfield
Talat Farooqi
John T. Plunket

DECEMBER 2002

Prepared under MMS Contract
14-35-0001-30660-19961
by
Coastal Fisheries Institute
Louisiana State University
Baton Rouge, LA 70803

Published by

U.S. Department of the Interior
Minerals Management Service
Gulf of Mexico OCS Region

Cooperative Agreement
Coastal Marine Institute
Louisiana State University

DISCLAIMER

This report was prepared under contract between the Minerals Management Service (MMS) and the Coastal Fisheries Institute (CFI), Louisiana State University (LSU). This report has been technically reviewed by the MMS and it has been approved for publication. Approval does not signify that the contents necessarily reflect the views and policies of LSU or the MMS, nor does mention of trades names or commercial products constitute endorsement or recommendation for use. It is, however, exempt from review and compliance with the MMS editorial standard.

REPORT AVAILABILITY

Extra copies of the report may be obtained from the Public Information Office (Mail Stop 5034) at the following address:

U.S. Department of the Interior
Minerals Management Service
Gulf of Mexico OCS Region
Public Information Office (MS 5034)
1201 Elmwood Boulevard
New Orleans, Louisiana 70123-2394

Telephone: (504) 736-2519 or
              1-800-200-GULF

CITATION

Suggested Citation:

Shaw, R.F., D.C. Lindquist, M.C. Benfield, T. Farooqi and J.T. Plunket. 2001. Offshore Petroleum Platforms: Functional Significance for Larval Fish Across Longitudinal and Latitudinal Gradients. Prepared by the Coastal Fisheries Institute, Louisiana State University. U.S. Department of the Interior, Minerals Management Service, Gulf of Mexico OCS Region, New Orleans, LA. OCS Study MMS 2002-077. 107 pp.

ACKNOWLEDGMENTS

We gratefully acknowledge funding by the Minerals Management Service-Louisiana State University-Coastal Marine Institute (Contract Number 30660-19961, OSR Number 10483). We thank Jason Box, Danny Cline, Landon Franklin, Robin Hargroder, Sean Keenan, Brian Milan, Rishi Ramtahal, Paul Rogers, and Christopher Whatley for their assistance in the field and laboratory. We are indebted to James Ditty, Joseph Cope and Frank Hernandez, Jr. for their efforts during our previous platform research, and during the initial stages of this study. We gratefully acknowledge the assistance of Drs. Ann Scarborough-Bull, Charles Wilson and David Stanley. We would also like to thank the Santa Fe-Snyder Oil Corporation and Murphy Oil for access to their offshore oil and gas platforms and logistical support, and the crews of Santa Fe-Snyder's MP 259A and Murphy Oil's VK 203 for their assistance and hospitality.

EXECUTIVE SUMMARY

The introduction and proliferation of offshore oil and gas platforms in the northern Gulf of Mexico (Gulf) has undoubtedly affected the marine ecosystem. There are approximately 4,000 platforms in the federal waters of the Gulf. Because a mud/silt/sand bottom with little relief or hard-substrate dominates the northern Gulf, especially west of the Mississippi River Delta (Delta), any additional hard-substrate provided by platforms could prove significant. Although platforms provide an estimated 11.7 km^2 (or 0.4%) of the total "reef" habitat in the northern Gulf, platform significance may be enhanced by the vertical relief of their substrate, which extends from the bottom through the photic zone to the surface. Because fish populations are usually limited by available energy, recruitment, or habitat, it is important to determine if platforms: 1) serve as new or additional spawning habitat; 2) provide critical habitat for early life history stages; or 3) influence energy flow through the ecosystem by aggregating prey.

Some researchers believe that certain reef fish species may be experiencing nursery habitat limitation, i.e., the availability of shelter at the time of settlement is the limiting factor for reef fish populations. Therefore, an underlying rationale for artificial reef deployment is that they provide critical habitat for settling reef fishes, and, subsequently, improve recruitment and adult production. Despite research efforts, however, biologists still disagree over the paradigm of whether artificial reefs contribute significantly to new fish production or simply attract and concentrate individuals from surrounding habitats. Because the north-central Gulf has little reef habitat, it is likely that the contribution of artificial reefs (e.g., platforms) has enhanced reef fish populations, although the net impact of this augmentation is unknown.

Few baseline, ecological ichthyoplankton studies within the Gulf's offshore oil and gas fields have been published, and, therefore, the role that platforms may play as essential fish habitat has not been adequately addressed. This study focused on three objectives designed to evaluate the ecological significance of platforms to the early life history stages of fishes. The first objective was to characterize the larval and juvenile fish assemblages at two platforms east of the Delta. Data from these collections were analyzed with data collected previously from three platforms west of the Delta to determine whether there were differences in the larval and juvenile fish assemblages at platforms by depth (across-shelf) and by east/west of the Delta (along-shelf), as seen for adult populations. The second objective was to assess how platforms affect the local distribution and abundance of larval and juvenile fishes, and, therefore, whether platforms have a nursery/refugia function for fishes. The third objective was to provide much needed ecological information on the early life history stages of reef fishes, e.g., seasonality, lunar periodicity, horizontal distribution, and relative abundance.

Larval and juvenile fishes were sampled at two platforms east of the Delta. Santa Fe-Snyder's Main Pass (MP) 259, which stands in 120 m of water on the outer shelf (29°19'32" N, 88°01'12" W), was sampled over two-night periods, twice monthly (i.e., new and full moon phases) during May-September 1999. Murphy Oil's Viosca Knoll (VK) 203, which stands in 35 m of water at mid-shelf (29°46'53" N, 88°19'59" W), was also sampled over two-night periods, twice monthly during May-October 2000. These platforms were selected to complement and supplement previous sampling efforts at platforms west of the Delta [i.e., the inner shelf platform South Timbalier (ST) 54, the mid-shelf platform Grand Isle (GI) 94, and the outer shelf platform

Green Canyon (GC) 18]. Larval and juvenile fishes were collected within the platform structure using passive plankton nets and light traps fished at the surface, and off-platform (about 20 m down-current of the platform) using light traps. Data collected from MP 259 and VK 203 were analyzed with data from the three platforms west of the Delta.

Patterns of larval and juvenile fish abundance and diversity were primarily influenced by across-shelf gradients of increasing water depth. Larval fish total densities from plankton nets were highest for the inner shelf platform ST 54, and decreased with increasing depth. Light trap total CPUEs were highest for the mid-shelf platforms VK 203 and GI 94, and were generally low at the outer shelf platforms. Diversity and taxonomic richness were both generally greatest at the mid-shelf platforms. This higher diversity and abundance of postlarval and juvenile fishes at the mid-shelf platforms may be attributed to an overlap in species distributions between coastal and oceanic/tropical taxa. Furthermore, the platforms at intermediate depth may have higher diversity because they reside in areas of highest platform concentration, i.e., more potential up-current sources of larvae.

The species composition of the non-clupeiform larval and juvenile fish assemblages at platforms also seemed to be structured by depth. Cluster analysis found three general assemblages: an inner shelf assemblage (ST 54), a mid-shelf assemblage (GI 94 and VK 203) and an outer shelf assemblage (GC 18 and MP 259). High densities of sciaenids, synodontids and other coastal taxa characterized the inner shelf assemblage. The mid-shelf assemblage was characterized by blenniids, synodontids, and *Bregmaceros cantori*. The mid-shelf platforms also had the highest abundance and diversity of reef fishes, particularly blenniids, lutjanids, and pomacentrids. The outer shelf assemblage was primarily composed of oceanic pelagic taxa, such as carangids and scombrids, and mesopelagic taxa. Because they generally agree with those found for adult populations, the assemblages observed at platforms probably reflect adult spawning behavior. The only differences observed in the larval and juvenile fish assemblages across longitudinal gradients (i.e., east or west of the Delta) were differences in the abundance of certain taxa. The higher abundances of these taxa collected at platforms east or west of the Delta may be attributed to the dominant hydrographic conditions and the availability of habitat in the northeastern and northwestern Gulf.

The waters within platforms had higher abundance and diversity of postlarval and juvenile fishes than waters immediately down-current of the platform. Clupeiforms (clupeids and engraulids) and synodontids were consistently collected in higher abundance within the platform than off-platform. Taxa collected primarily in waters down-current of the platforms included scombrids and possibly carangids. These taxa are highly predatory and, therefore, may be utilizing the concentrations of zooplankton and ichthyoplankton that are attracted to the light field of platforms. Reef fish were occasionally found in higher abundance within-platform, yet pomacentrids and the blenniid *Hypsoblennius invemar* were often found in higher abundance off-platform. These specimens, though, were collected at settlement-size and may represent individuals settling to the platform. The few differences observed between the "background" continental shelf (SEAMAP) collections and platform abundances of reef taxa were confounded by the large disparity in sampling effort between SEAMAP and platform samples. In general, blenniids and pomacentrids were more abundant in platform plankton nets and light traps, while serranids and lutjanids were more abundant in SEAMAP bongo nets and neuston nets.

The larval and juvenile reef fishes collected at platforms exhibited distinct temporal patterns of abundance. Most of the reef taxa were collected during months when surface water temperatures were at their highest, i.e., June-August. The exceptions were the serranid subfamilies Anthinae and Serraninae, which were predominantly collected during the late spring and early fall, respectively. There were strong differences in the numbers and developmental stages collected between new and full moons. Many preflexion reef larvae (larval stages before the onset of caudal fin development) were collected in higher numbers on new moons, but preflexion holocentrids, labrids and some blenniids were collected predominantly on full moons. Postflexion reef larvae, however, were almost exclusively collected on new moons, which was consistent with peak periods of settlement for many reef fishes. Coefficients of variation, calculated from the mean plankton net and light trap catches per sampling night and sampling trip, indicated pulses in the catches of several dominant taxa at platforms. Light trap-collected blenniids and pomacentrids, in particular, were primarily found in very discrete pulses containing the majority of settlement-size fishes collected at platforms. The occurrence of these pulses during darker periods of the lunar month (i.e., first quarter and new moons) further suggests that they were settlement-related. Settlement pulses, comprising the majority of a given year class, have been observed for many species of reef fish.

Examination of the length frequency and developmental stages of reef taxa collected at platforms provided indirect evidence of the potential spawning and nursery/recruitment habitat provided by platforms. Recently-hatched and preflexion blenniid, holocentrids, labrid, lutjanid, scarid, and serranid larvae were collected at every platform, indicating near by (recent) spawning. Although it is possible that these larvae were spawned at natural reefs, the preponderance of platforms within the transport envelope of these larvae, and the general absence of natural hard bottoms off central Louisiana, make platforms the most probable source. Blenniids and pomacentrids were the most abundant settlement-size reef taxa. Settlement-size larvae of other reef taxa were relatively rare, as compared with blenniids and pomacentrids, and were represented mostly by lutjanids, particularly at the mid-shelf platforms. The relative abundance of settlement-size reef larvae at platforms may be influenced by two disparate spawning strategies exhibited by reef fishes: broadcast spawning of pelagic eggs or benthic spawning of demersal adhesive eggs. Pelagic spawners, e.g., serranids and labrids, generally have larvae with longer larval durations that are more susceptible to predation and advective loss. Meanwhile, benthic spawners, e.g., blenniids and pomacentrids, generally have larvae with shorter larval durations and limited dispersal, and, thus, may be able to remain in areas where suitable settlement habitat is more available.

Environmental conditions influenced the abundance of larval and juvenile fishes collected at both MP 259 and VK 203. Seasonal variations in temperature influenced the abundances of several taxa at the outer shelf platform MP 259. Several taxa were also associated with different water masses that occurred at MP 259. There was less environmental variability at the mid-shelf platform VK 203, and consequently microzooplankton biomass was the most influential environmental variable for larval and juvenile fish abundances. Catch efficiency of the gear was also affected by the prevailing environmental conditions. Light trap efficiency was impaired by high water current conditions with CPUEs <10 fish/10 min at current speeds greater than 30 cm s^{-1}. At these current speeds, the catch was predominantly preflexion larvae (median length <10 mm) that were passively entrained by the gear. Larger postlarvae and juveniles were seemingly relatively unavailable to light traps at the highest current speeds, probably due to their inability to maneuver to and enter the light trap at these current speeds.

This study represents an important step towards understanding the ecological significance of oil and gas platforms to the early life history stages of fishes. Platforms represent hard-substrate (i.e., "vertical benthos") imposed on the pelagic environment. However, the most common postlarval and juvenile fishes collected at platforms represented species that are pelagic as adults, e.g., clupeiforms, carangids and scombrids, and the presettlement stages of soft-bottom taxa, e.g., synodontids. Populations of these taxa may benefit from increased foraging opportunities provided by concentrations of prey that may be found in the waters around platforms. Platforms may also provide nursery/recruitment habitat for certain reef taxa, i.e., blenniids and pomacentrids. Because artificial reefs most likely benefit species that are habitat-limited, platforms should enhance the production of typical shallow water reef taxa (e.g., blenniids and pomacentrids) by providing additional spawning habitat and, to a much lesser extent, nursery/recruitment habitat.

TABLE OF CONTENTS

LIST OF FIGURES

LIST OF TABLES

Introduction

The introduction and proliferation of offshore oil and gas platforms (hereafter referred to as platforms) in the northern Gulf of Mexico (Gulf) has undoubtedly affected the marine ecosystem. There are approximately 4,000 platforms in the federal waters of the Gulf (Stanley and Wilson 2000). Because a mud/silt/sand bottom with little relief or hard-substrate dominates the northern Gulf, especially west of the Mississippi River Delta (Delta), any additional hard-substrate provided by platforms could prove significant. Although platforms provide an estimated 11.7 km^2 (or 0.4%) of the total "reef" habitat in the northern Gulf (Gallaway 1999), platform significance may be enhanced by the vertical relief of their substrate, which extends from the bottom through the photic zone to the surface. Because fish populations are usually limited by available energy, recruitment, or habitat, it is important to determine if platforms: 1) serve as new or additional spawning habitat; 2) provide critical habitat for early life history stages; or 3) influence energy flow through the ecosystem by aggregating prey.

Platforms can enhance fisheries by providing attachment substrate for habitat-limited sessile invertebrates, thereby creating food and habitat for reef-dependent species that are trophically dependent on these invertebrates (Gallaway 1981; Bohnsack and Sutherland 1985; Bohnsack 1991). In addition, platforms may offer refugia for species that are trophically independent of the biofouling community, but are ecologically important resident, seasonal, or transient members of the fish community (Gallaway and Martin 1980). Less well known, however, is whether platforms provide additional spawning habitat for fishes. Direct evidence of spawning by resident fishes is difficult to obtain because of the patchiness of eggs and yolk-sac larvae, the likelihood of significant and variable advection to and away from platforms by passive pelagic forms, and the inaccessibility of demersal/adhesive eggs. However, at least one species, the sergeant-major damselfish *Abudefduf saxatilis*, has been observed guarding nests on platform structure (Scarborough-Bull and Kendall 1994). Spawning has also been observed on other types of artificial reefs (Pickering and Whitmarsh 1997). Therefore, it is likely that reproduction does occur at platforms, particularly for demersal spawners such as blenniids and pomacentrids (Bohnsack 1989; Pickering and Whitmarsh 1997).

Because larval supply can often exceed the numbers able to settle on a reef, some researchers believe that larval supply and mortality during the planktonic stage may limit adult reef fish populations (Sale 1980; Victor 1983). However, others believe that some species of fish may be experiencing nursery habitat limitation, i.e., the availability of shelter at the time of settlement is the limiting factor (Ursin 1982; Shulman 1985; Hixon and Beets 1989). In the absence of suitable shelter, the time of settlement for postlarval fishes is often characterized by high predation rates by resident populations. An underlying rationale for artificial reef deployment is that they provide critical habitat for early life history stages and, subsequently, improve recruitment and adult production (Bohnsack 1989; Bohnsack et al. 1994).

Despite the potential for increased reef fish recruitment, biologists still disagree over the paradigm of whether artificial reefs contribute significantly to new fish production or simply attract and concentrate individuals from surrounding habitats, thereby making them potentially more vulnerable to harvest (Pickering and Whitmarsh 1997; Bortone 1998). Bohnsack (1989) theorized that reef effects fell along a continuum between attraction and production. Species most likely to benefit from increased productivity are habitat-limited, territorial, obligatory reef species. The attraction hypothesis is more likely in areas where natural reef habitat is abundant and where species are recruitment-limited, highly mobile, and opportunistic reef species. Because the north-central Gulf has little reef habitat, it is likely that the contribution of artificial reefs (e.g., platforms) has enhanced reef fish populations, although the net impact of this augmentation is unknown.

Few baseline ichthyoplankton studies within the oil field have been published (Finucane et al. 1979a; Finucane et al. 1979b; Bedinger et al. 1980) and none have been published that focus on platform infrastructure. The National Marine Fisheries Service (NMFS)/Southeastern Area Monitoring and Assessment Program's (SEAMAP) Gulf-wide fisheries surveys and the Minerals Management Service Louisiana-Texas (MMS LATEX) Physical Oceanography Program have historically not sampled in the immediate vicinity of platforms because of conservative navigation/safety requirements. Therefore, fisheries-independent assessment of the abundance of fish early life history stages within and immediately around these platforms and the role they might play as essential fish habitat has not been adequately addressed.

The adult fish assemblages on natural and artificial reefs (including platforms), however, are well known and often associated with water depth in the northern Gulf (Hastings 1976; Sonnier et al. 1976; Stanley and Wilson 2000). Demersal fish assemblages have been divided into depth zones corresponding to the distribution of major shrimp species (i.e., white shrimp grounds: 3-22 m depth, brown shrimp grounds: 22-110 m depth; Chittenden and McEachern 1976). Using this information, Gallaway (1981) described distinct transitions between reef and platform fish assemblages across these depths. Overall, the outer shelf (>60 m depth) reefs and platforms seemed to be more speciose, followed by the mid-shelf (20-60 m) and the inner shelf (3-20m). More tropical taxa were present at the outer shelf, such as haemulids, labrids and scarids. There was some overlap between reef species at the outer and mid-shelf habitats, but in general, tropical taxa were replaced by more temperate species, such as serranids and sparids, at the shallower sites. This transition was presumably due to cooler winter temperatures limiting the distribution of tropical species at inshore habitats.

In addition to depth-related (across-shelf) transitions, differences in adult fish assemblages east and west of the Delta (along-shelf) have been noted in the northern Gulf and have been attributed to substrate characteristics and circulation patterns (Briggs 1958; Chittenden and McEachern 1976; Hoese and Moore 1998). Terrigeneous muds from the Mississippi and Atchafalaya Rivers are predominant in the northwestern Gulf, while sand, biogenic calcareous sediments and limestone outcroppings are more common east of the Delta (Parker 1960; Chittenden and McEachern 1976). The Mississippi River discharge, which predominantly is a westerly flow from the Delta, and the Loop Current, which brings Caribbean waters into the Gulf, dominate the circulation patterns in the Gulf. The large volume of freshwater leaving the Mississippi River distributaries may present a barrier to the dispersal of certain coastal taxa (Hildebrand 1954; McClure and McEachern 1992). Although the Loop Current, by way of shedding warm-core rings, may seed offshore reefs in the northwestern Gulf with Caribbean postlarval/juvenile fish, it generally favors eastward dispersal of these taxa (Shipp 1992). This combination of circulation and more favorable reef-type habitats, along with warmer and more saline hydrographic conditions, has resulted in tropical reef fish species being more common in the northeastern Gulf (Briggs 1958; Smith 1976).

This study focused on three objectives designed to evaluate the ecological significance of oil and gas platforms to the early life history stages of fishes. The first objective was to characterize the larval and juvenile fish assemblages within and immediately around two platforms east of the Delta. Data from these collections were analyzed with data collected previously from three platforms west of the Delta (Hernandez 2001; Hernandez et al. 2001; Hernandez et al. in press) to determine whether there were significant differences in the larval and juvenile fish assemblages by depth (across-shelf) and by east/west of the Delta (along-shelf) as found for adult populations in the northern Gulf. The second objective was to assess how platforms affect the local distribution and abundance of larval and juvenile fishes. Near-field collections within the platform infrastructure were compared with synoptic data taken from waters 20 m down-current from the platform, and from background data taken further afield (i.e., SEAMAP data). The third objective was to provide much needed ecological information on the early life history stages of reef fishes, e.g., seasonality, lunar periodicity and large-scale distribution patterns, and to address whether platforms have a nursery/refugia function for these fishes. Unlike the majority of species in ichthyoplankton collections (e.g., soft-bottom or pelagic species), reef/hard-bottom species are often associated with platforms as adults, and, therefore, populations of these fishes may benefit from the increased habitat provided by platforms. Reef fishes were classified as either reef-dependent or reef-associated (Choat and Bellwood 1991). Reef-dependent taxa are those that are associated with reef habitat for the duration of their adult life and included individuals from the families: Acanthuridae (surgeonfishes), Chaetodontidae (butterflyfishes), Labridae (wrasses), Pomacanthidae (angelfishes), Pomacentridae (damselfishes), and Scaridae (parrotfishes). Reef-associated taxa are those that exploit the resources of the reef but also occur in other habitats. Although this definition could encompass certain pelagic (e.g., Carangidae, Scombridae and Sphyraenidae) and benthic taxa (Gobiidae, Muraenidae and Synodontidae), we focused on the families: Blenniidae (blennies), Holocentridae (squirrelfishes), Lutjanidae (snappers), and Serranidae (sea basses).

Materials and Methods

Study Areas

Larval and juvenile fishes were sampled at two platforms east of the Delta: Santa Fe-Snyder's Main Pass (MP) 259 and Murphy Oil's Viosca Knoll (VK) 203 (Figure 1). These platforms were selected based on characterizations of the adult fish assemblages by Gallaway and Martin (1980), Gallaway (1981) and Continental Shelf Associates (1982) who reported that nektonic communities around platforms could be categorized by water depth in the northern Gulf. These platforms were also selected to complement and supplement previous sampling efforts at platforms west of the Delta (Hernandez et al. 2001). Main Pass 259 (29°19'32" N, 88°01'12" W; installed in 1994), which stands in about 120 m of water on the outer shelf, was sampled twice monthly from May to September 1999. Viosca Knoll 203 (29°46'53" N, 88°19'59" W; installed in 1993), which stands in about 35 m of water at mid-shelf, was sampled twice monthly from May to October 2000. Inclement weather forced the cancellation of one trip in early August and two trips during September at VK 203. Furthermore, the October trip took place during the moon's first quarter. Both platforms have similar structural complexity; MP 259 is a six-pile (or leg) platform, and while VK 203 has four piles it also has a well deck that extends from the platform's north side and down to about 10 m depth, creating *de facto* fifth and six piles in the upper water column.

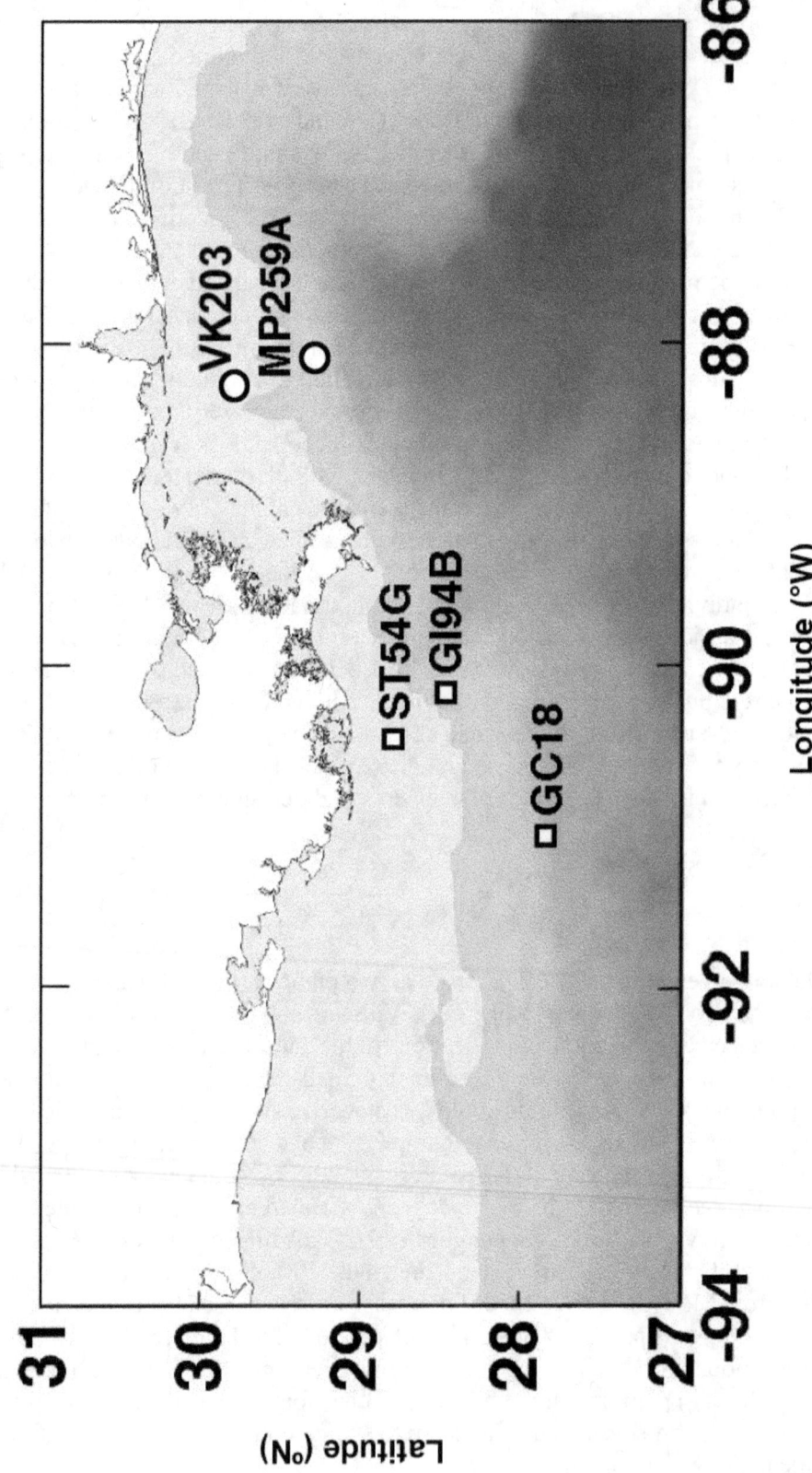

Figure 1. Location of oil and gas platforms sampled in the northern Gulf of Mexico. Circles represent platforms sampled during the present study. Squares represent platforms sampled during previous studies, used for comparisons.

Sampling Procedures

Sampling protocols at MP 259 and VK 203 were similar to those conducted at platforms west of the Delta (Hernandez et al. 2001). Samples were taken over two consecutive nights at approximately 14-day intervals coincident with new and full moon phases (Table 1). These moon phases were targeted because they have been associated with either peak spawning or recruitment periods for many reef-dependent fishes (Johannes 1978; Robertson et al. 1988). The main sampling station for each platform was located in the internal central region along a stainless-steel guidewire tethered to the first set of the platform's underwater cross-member support structures. At this station, larval and juvenile fish collections were made using a near-surface modified quatrefoil light trap with power supplied via an umbilical connected to a 12-volt marine battery (Hernandez et al. 2001 for specifications), and a near-surface, passively-fished, 60-cm diameter plankton net (333 µm mesh, dyed dark green) rigged with a flow meter (General Oceanics flowmeter 2030 with slow velocity rotor). In addition, collections were made using a light trap that was tethered and free-drifted away from the platform (off-platform) to a distance of 20 m on the down-current side of the platform. All light traps were deployed with their lights off, fished with their lights on and retrieved with their lights off. Each of these gears was sampled during four sets each night, with two sets taken before midnight and two sets taken after midnight. The order of light trap and plankton net collections was randomized within each set. Also, on three occasions during July and August 2000 at VK 203, samples were collected with light traps deployed at three distances relative to the platform: within the platform; 20 m down-current from the platform; and 50 m down-current from the platform.

Temperature (°C), salinity (ppt) and turbidity (NTU) were measured during each set using a Hydrolab DataSonde 3. Current speed and direction were recorded using an InterOcean S4 Current Meter. During each set a plankton net (30-cm, 63 µm mesh), which was held rigidly to the guidewire, was lowered cod-end first to the bottom of the guidewire, left at depth for 5 minutes for water column restabilization, then hauled vertically to the surface at about 1m/s to ascertain microzooplankton biomass as a measure of prey availability. The resulting samples were filtered through a pre-weighed, microfiber filter (1.2 µm), dried in an oven for 24 hr at 60°C, then weighed to determine the dry weight biomass (g m^{-3}). Surface water samples were also collected during each set to determine total suspended solids, an estimate of turbidity. These samples were filtered, dried, and weighed to determine the suspended sediment load (g/500 ml).

Samples of larval and juvenile fishes were preserved in 10% buffered formaldehyde and changed over to ethanol within 8-12 hours. Fish were removed from all samples, enumerated and identified to the lowest possible taxonomic level using the taxonomic classification of Robins et al. (1991). Fish were measured under a dissecting microscope with the aid of an ocular micrometer. Preflexion larvae were measured to the end of the notochord (notochord length: NL) and postflexion larvae and juveniles were measured to the end of the vertebral column (standard length: SL). In the event that the number of fish in a sample was greater than 50 for any single species, the largest, smallest and a random subsample of 50 individuals was measured. Light trap samples were standardized to a catch-per-unit-effort (CPUE) of fish per 10 min. Plankton net samples were standardized to the number of fish per 100 m^3 (density).

Table 1. Number of samples collected by date and gear for both platforms east of the Mississippi River Delta. (Lunar phases: N= new moon; F= full moon).

	Off-platform Light Trap	Surface Light Trap	Surface Plankton Net
Main Pass 259A (1999)			
May 29-30 (F)	0	6	6
Jun 12-14 (N)	8	8	8
Jun 26-28 (F)	0	8	8
Jul 10-12 (N)	8	8	8
Jul 26-28 (F)	8	8	8
Aug 10-12 (N)	8	8	8
Aug 24-26 (F)	8	8	8
Sep 7-9 (N)	8	8	8
Sep 24-26 (F)	8	8	8
Totals	**56**	**70**	**70**
Viosca Knoll 203 (2000)			
May 18-20 (F)	8	8	8
May 31-Jun 2 (N)	8	8	8
Jun 14-16 (F)	8	8	8
Jun 29-Jul 1 (N)	8	8	8
Jul 15-17 (F)	8	8	8
Jul 30-Aug 1 (N)	8	8	8
Aug 29-31 (N)	8	8	8
Oct 6-7 ‡	4	4	4
Totals	**60**	**60**	**60**

‡ samples taken during first quarter moon.

Data Analyses

Data collected at MP 259 and VK 203 were compared with data previously collected at platforms west of the Delta, i.e., the inner shelf platform South Timbalier (ST) 54, the mid-shelf platform Grand Isle (GI) 94 and the outer shelf platform Green Canyon (GC) 18 (Hernandez et al. 2001). To avoid bias, only data from common sampling periods and sampling gears were included in the analyses, i.e., data from months other than May through August and from subsurface light traps and plankton nets were dropped. Because most of the data sets analyzed were non-normal in their distribution, nonparametric Kruskal-Wallis ANOVAs ($\alpha = 0.05$) were used to compare mean total plankton net densities, light trap CPUEs and Shannon-Wiener diversity indices (Magurran 1988) from each platform. Nonparametric Tukey-type multiple comparison tests were used to determine which means were significantly different (Zar 1984). Because very large numbers of clupeiforms overwhelmed the trends of other taxa collected at the platforms, these analyses were run with and without clupeiforms included. These and subsequent analyses were performed using SAS version 6.12 (SAS Institute, Inc. 1989) unless otherwise noted.

Similarity among the non-clupeiform larval and juvenile fish assemblages of each platform was calculated using the Bray-Curtis index of similarity (= 1 – Bray-Curtis dissimilarity; Krebs 1999). Fish collections from all gears, from May through August, were combined for each platform and the relative contribution of each taxon to the total non-clupeiform catch was calculated. In general, only fishes identified to at least the genus level were included in this analysis, however, unidentified Gobiidae and Myctophidae were also included because they were numerically dominant at certain platforms. Each platform assemblage was compared with every other platform assemblage and the resulting similarity matrix was used to create a cluster diagram using the group-average sorting method in SYSTAT version 9 (SPSS, Inc. 1999). The resulting dendrogram ordered platforms into groups of similarly structured fish assemblages.

Mean plankton net densities and light trap CPUEs of the dominant fish taxa collected at platforms were statistically compared relative to their collection east or west of the Delta. Samples taken at MP 259 and VK 203 were categorized as east Delta, while samples taken at GC 18, GI 94 and ST54 were categorized as west Delta. Only samples taken from surface waters during the months of May through August were included in this analysis. Means were compared using the nonparametric Wilcoxon 2-sample test (Zar 1984).

The potential effect of platforms on the distribution and abundance of postlarval and juvenile fishes was examined by comparing light trap catches from the surface waters within-platform vs. off-platform at each platform (east and west of the Delta). Wilcoxon 2-sample tests were used to compare mean total light trap CPUEs and Shannon-Wiener diversity indices between locations. Similar analyses were run on the CPUEs of dominant taxa (including clupeiform taxa) and reef fish families collected at each platform. Kruskal-Wallis ANOVAs were used to compare the mean total CPUEs and diversity indices collected between the within-platform, and the 20 m and 50 m off-platform light trap samples collected at VK 203. Kolmogorov-Smirnov (K-S) length frequency analyses were performed for selected taxa ($n \geq 10$ for each gear) at each platform to determine if there were differences in the size distributions of these taxa collected within- vs. off-platform. All K-S tests were performed using SYSTAT version 9 (SPSS, Inc. 1999).

Platform-collected reef fish larval abundances were compared to open-water or "background" abundances from nearby SEAMAP surveys. Data were selected from SEAMAP sampling stations, from data sets for the years 1995-1997 (the most recent available data sets), that were relatively close in both proximity (location on shelf) and water depth to each platform, and during the same months as platform collections (i.e., April-August). Oblique bongo net (60-cm diameter; 333 μm mesh) and neuston net (1 x 2 m mouth; 948 μm mesh) samples were collected at these stations using standard SEAMAP protocols (SEAMAP 2000). Because abundances from bongo nets were expressed as fish per 10 m^2, abundances from paired passive plankton nets (surface and subsurface) at platforms were standardized using the equation:

$$[(N_1 + N_2)/(V_1 + V_2)] \times D \times 10$$

where: N_1 = number of fish in surface sample
N_2 = number of fish in subsurface sample
V_1 = volume of water filtered by surface net
V_2 = volume of water filtered by subsurface net
D = total depth sampled.

Because subsurface plankton nets were not used at platforms east of the Delta, flowmeter readings from the oblique bongo tows were used to calculate densities of fish per 100 m^3. Mean abundances from bongo tows were then compared with mean abundances from plankton nets at platforms for reef fish families. Similarly, the mean number of reef fish taxa collected in SEAMAP neuston net samples was compared with the mean number collected in light trap samples (within- and off-platform combined) for each platform. No statistical comparisons were attempted due to differences in sampling effort and protocols between SEAMAP and platform data. However, reef fish size distributions were compared between bongo nets and plankton nets, and neuston nets and light traps, using K-S tests (<10 individuals for each gear).

The frequency of reef fishes collected during new vs. full moons was compared, from all platforms combined (except GC 18 where sampling occurred only on new moons), using chi-square goodness of fit tests ($\alpha = 0.01$; Zar 1984). To distinguish between possible spawning and settlement events, separate analyses were performed for the total numbers of preflexion and postflexion fish collected on new and full moons at platforms. Published data were used to make the distinction between these developmental stages. Because the total number of samples (plankton nets and light traps combined) taken on new moons was higher than on full moons (n= 714 and 527, respectively), the expected frequencies for each chi-square analysis were similarly disproportional (58:42, new: full).

Several studies have noted that spawning and recruitment often occur in pulses of short duration (Robertson et al. 1988; Doherty 1991). To identify taxa that exhibited pulses at platforms, coefficients of variation (CVs; standardized to 100%) were calculated from the mean densities and CPUEs among trips and among nights within a sampling season for the ten most abundant non-clupeiforms in plankton nets and light traps, and for abundant families of reef fish. These analyses were performed for data from GI 94 and VK 203, because these platforms had the highest numbers of reef fish collected. Plots of the nightly mean density and CPUE for taxa were used, in combination with the coefficients of variation, to further illustrate the variability in catch, i.e., the taxa with the highest CVs should exhibit the most discrete pulse.

Temporal variability in larval and juvenile fish abundance was also analyzed within nights. Mean total plankton net densities and light trap CPUEs were calculated for each hour that sampling occurred after sunset at each platform. These means were compared using the Kruskal-Wallis ANOVA and Tukey's tests. Similar tests were performed on the hourly mean densities and CPUEs of the most abundant non-clupeiform fish taxa and reef fish families.

Canonical correlations were used to determine relationships between larval and juvenile fish abundance and environmental variables at MP 259 and VK 203. Log-transformed $(\log_{10}(x+1))$ plankton net densities and light trap CPUEs of the top 15 non-clupeiform taxa, and reef fish families, were analyzed along with temperature, salinity, microzooplankton biomass and measurements of turbidity. The importance of an environmental variable was based on the magnitude of its correlation with the environmental variate, with the sign of the correlation indicating if the variable was directly or inversely related with the variate. A taxa was considered to be related to the variate if the absolute value of the correlation was greater than 0.387 (i.e., the variate predicted ≥15% of the species' variation within the model).

The effect of current speed on light trap catches was assessed by plotting the mean total light trap CPUE against current speed (cm s^{-1}), as measured by the S4 Current Meter. Because there was no obvious difference in the relationship of light trap CPUE vs. current speed depending on the location of the light trap (within- vs. off-platform), the mean light trap CPUE per set (from both light traps combined) was plotted against the mean current speed during that set. These means were calculated from MP 259 and VK 203 and the results from both platforms were combined. The size distributions of fishes collected at different current levels, from both MP 259 and VK 203 combined, were analyzed using K-S tests.

Results

Environmental Characterization of Sampling Sites

Environmental conditions were variable at the outer shelf platform MP 259 (Figure 2). Mean surface temperatures increased over the season from 27.8 °C in May to a peak of 31.5 °C during late August, and then decreased to a low of 27.7 °C during late September. Although surface salinities ranged from 29-34 ppt during most of the sampling season, minimums were seen in May and late August (26.7 and 23.5 ppt, respectively). Mean surface turbidities ranged from 0.2 to 2.5 NTU, while microzooplankton biomass ranged from 0.2 to 1.4 g m^{-3}. Peaks in mean turbidity and microzooplankton biomass coincided with the lower salinities observed during May and late August, which suggests the presence offshore of river plume water.

In contrast, most environmental variables were relatively stable at the mid-shelf platform VK 203 (Figure 3). Mean surface temperatures showed a similar seasonal pattern as at MP 259, with low temperatures during May (25.7 °C) and high temperatures during late August (30.2 °C). However, mean surface salinities showed very little variation, ranging from 31.6 to 33.5 ppt. Mean surface turbidity measurements from the Hydrolab were near zero at all times, except for

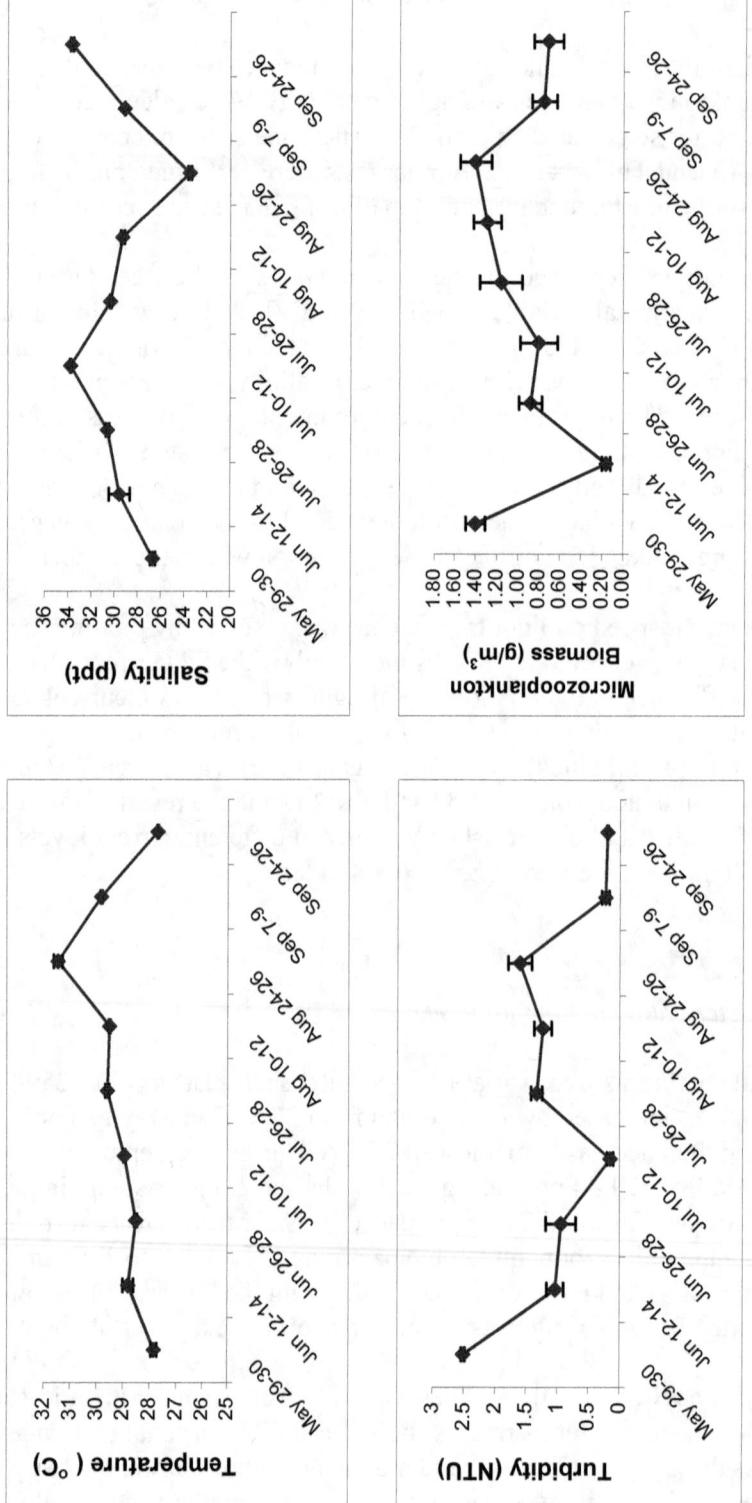

Figure 2. Mean surface temperatures, surface salinities, surface turbidities, and microzooplankton biomass (with standard errors) for each sampling trip at the outer shelf platform, MP 259 (depth = 120 m).

10

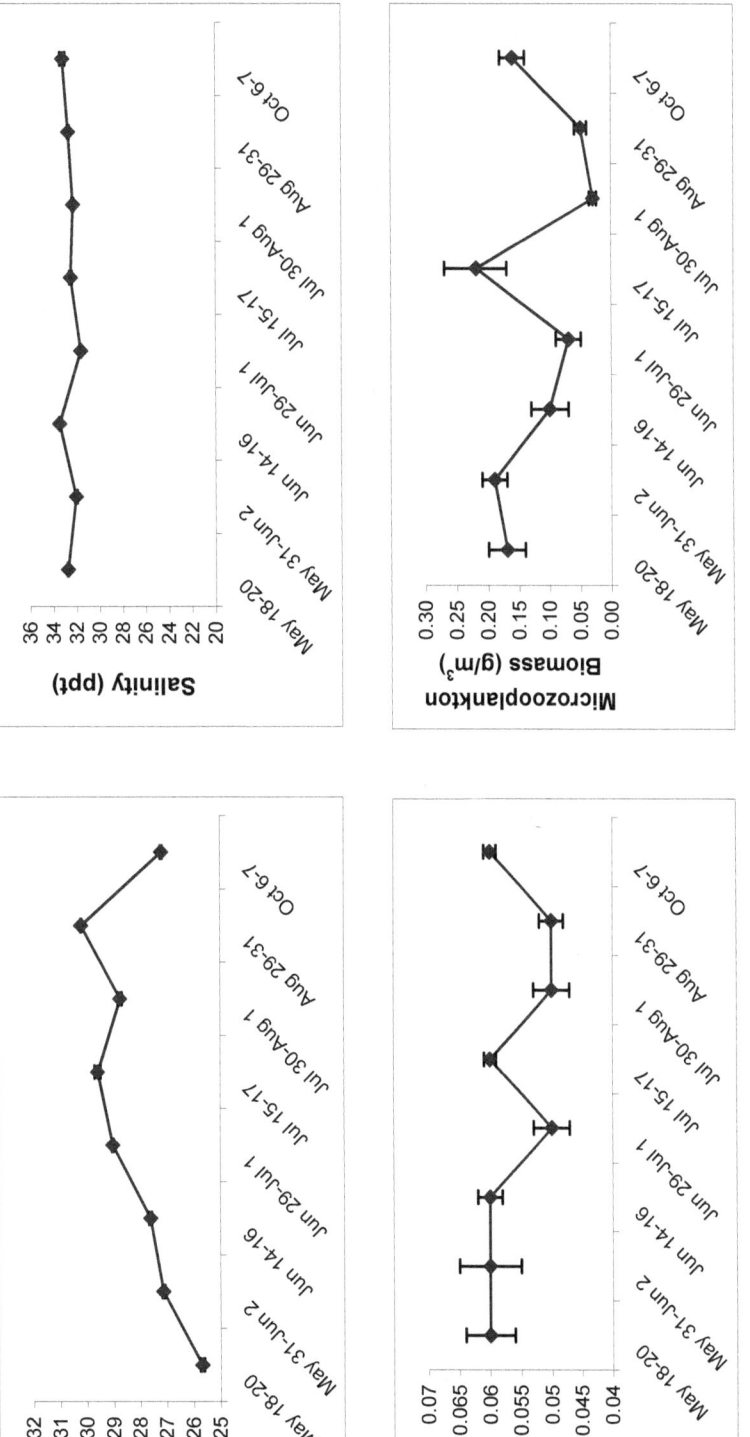

Figure 3. Mean surface temperatures, surface salinities, suspended solids, and microzooplankton biomass (with standard errors) for each sampling trip at the mid-shelf platform, VK 203 (depth = 35 m).

11

the nights of July 15-16 (mean turbidity = 1.8 NTU ± 0.05 SE) and October 6-7 (mean = 8.4 ± 0.13). Mean surface suspended solid concentrations were relatively stable, only ranging between 0.05-0.06 g/500 ml. Mean microzooplankton biomass was lower than at MP 259 and ranged from 0.03 to 0.2 g m^{-3}. Both the suspended solids and microzooplankton biomass curves showed similar patterns with lower values between June and August interrupted by a peak on July 15-17.

Characterization of Fish Catches at MP 259 and VK 203

A total of 16,439 fish, from 43 families and 69 taxa (identified to at least the genus level), was collected at the outer shelf platform MP 259 between May and September 1999 (Table 2). Of this total, 14,856 fish were collected in plankton nets and 1,583 in light traps. Plankton net collections represented 41 families and 62 taxa, with 23 families and 33 taxa being unique to this gear type. Meanwhile, light traps collected 21 families and 36 taxa, of which 3 families and 7 taxa were unique to light traps. Mean Shannon-Wiener diversity indices were significantly higher for plankton net collections (mean = 1.39 ± 0.07) than light trap collections (mean = 0.82 ± 0.05; Wilcoxon Z = 5.77, p<0.0001). Clupeiform fishes, primarily *Anchoa* spp., *Engraulis eurystole* and *Opisthonema oglinum*, dominated the catch for both plankton nets (85.6% of the total catch) and light traps (80.3%). *Caranx crysos, Auxis* spp., and unidentified gobiids and myctophids were the dominant non-clupeiforms in plankton nets, while *Caranx crysos, Hypsoblennius invemar, Synodus foetens* and *Euthynnus alletteratus* were common in light traps.

At the mid-shelf platform VK 203, a total of 6,196 fish was collected between May and October 2000, representing 38 families and 83 taxa (identified to at least the genus level; Table 3). Plankton nets collected 4,190 fish, while light traps collected 2,006 fish. Plankton nets collected individuals from 33 families and 68 taxa, with 7 families and 15 taxa unique to nets. Light traps collected 31 families and 68 taxa, with 5 families and 15 taxa collected only by light traps. Mean Shannon-Wiener diversity indices were not significantly different (light trap mean = 1.26 ± 0.05 vs. plankton net mean = 1.13 ± 0.08). Clupeiforms were not as dominant at VK 203 as at MP 259, comprising only 60.0% of the total plankton net catch and 31.9% of the total light trap catch. *Bregmaceros cantori, Cynoscion arenarius, Micropogonias undulatus*, and unidentified gobiids were among the dominant non-clupeiform taxa collected in plankton nets, while *Saurida brasiliensis, Synodus foetens, Decapterus punctatus, Hypsoblennius invemar*, and *Euthynnus alletteratus* were common in light trap collections.

Across- and Along-Shelf Characterization of Larval and Juvenile Fish Assemblages

Mean densities of larval fishes from surface plankton nets were highest at the inner shelf platform and decreased with increasing water depth (Figure 4). With clupeiforms included, mean densities were significantly different between platforms (Kruskal-Wallis χ^2 = 38.26, p<0.0001), with highest densities at the inner shelf (ST 54 = 5001.1 fish 100m^{-3} ± 2467.9) and lowest at the outer shelf (GC 18 = 180.1 ± 52.0; Figure 4a). When clupeiforms were excluded from the analysis, mean densities were significantly different (χ^2 = 33.66, p<0.0001) and the same across-shelf pattern was observed, although no significant differences were found between the inner shelf platform ST 54, and the two platforms east of the Delta, VK 203 and MP 259.

Table 2. Mean light trap CPUE (fish/10 min) and plankton net density (fish/100 m^3) for fish collected at Main Pass 259, with standard error (SE), rank based on CPUE or densities, and percent of total catch (%N). For ranks, tied values received the mean of the corresponding ranks. RA = reef associated taxa, RD = reef dependent taxa.

TAXA	Months Collected	Off-Platform Light Trap CPUE (SE) Rank (%N)	Within-Platform Light Trap CPUE (SE) Rank (%N)	Surface Plankton Net Density (SE) Rank (%N)
Osteichthyes				
Unidentified	Jul, Aug	0 (0)	0.01 (0.01) 36.5 (<1.0)	0.06 (0.06) 67 (<1.0)
Anguilliformes				
Muraenidae				
Unidentified (moray eels)	Aug	0 (0)	0 (0)	0.02 (0.02) 80 (<1.0)
Ophichthidae				
Ophichthus spp. (snake eels)	May, Jun, Jul, Sep	0.02 (0.02) 38 (<1.0)	0.01 (0.01) 36.5 (<1.0)	0.30 (0.11) 43 (<1.0)
Congridae				
Unidentified (conger eels)	Jun	0 (0)	0 (0)	0.10 (0.06) 56 (<1.0)
Clupeiformes				
Clupeidae				
Harengula jaguana (scaled sardine)	May, Jun, Jul, Aug	0.50 (0.23) 3 (5.5)	0.53 (0.34) 4 (3.5)	33.06 (10.65) 3 (6.1)
Opisthonema oglinum (Atlantic thread herring)	May, Jun, Jul, Aug, Sep	2.39 (0.83) 1 (27.0)	5.34 (1.74) 2 (34.7)	220.93 (82.81) 1 (64.52)
Engraulidae				
Unidentified	May, Jun, Jul, Aug, Sep	0.07 (0.03) 19.5 (<1.0)	0.14 (0.08) 10.5 (<1.0)	25.52 (12.34) 4 (5.1)
Anchoa spp.	May, Jun, Jul, Aug, Sep	0.21 (0.07) 7 (2.4)	0.11 (0.06) 14.5 (<1.0)	40.97 (13.84) 2 (8.4)
Anchoa cubana (Cuban anchovy)	Sep	0 (0)	0 (0)	0.11 (0.11) 53 (<1.0)
Anchoa hepsetus (striped anchovy)	May, Jul, Aug, Sep	0.48 (0.19) 4 (5.4)	0.14 (0.12) 10.5 (<1.0)	1.81 (0.92) 19 (<1.0)
Anchoa mitchilli (bay anchovy)	May, Jun, Jul, Aug, Sep	0.11 (0.07) 14 (1.2)	0.16 (0.09) 8 (1.1)	2.22 (0.93) 16 (<1.0)
Anchoa nasuta (longnose anchovy)	May, Jun, Jul, Aug, Sep	0.18 (0.08) 9 (2.0)	0.04 (0.02) 23.5 (<1.0)	3.40 (1.13) 12 (<1.0)
Anchoa nasuta/hepsetus (longnose/striped anchovy)	May, Jun, Jul, Sep	0.04 (0.03) 29.5 (<1.0)	0.29 (0.27) 5 (1.9)	2.98 (1.30) 15 (<1.0)
Anchoviella perfasciata (flat anchovy)	Aug, Sep	0.18 (0.08) 9 (2.0)	0.07 (0.05) 19.5 (<1.0)	0 (0)
Engraulis eurystole (silver anchovy)	May, Jun, Jul, Aug, Sep	2.38 (0.65) 2 (26.8)	5.98 (2.59) 1 (39.0)	5.08 (2.26) 9 (<1.0)
Stomiiformes				
Gonostomatidae				
Cyclothone spp. (bristlemouths)	Aug, Sep	0 (0)	0 (0)	0.09 (0.07) 59 (<1.0)

Table 2. Main Pass 259 (continued)

TAXA	Months Collected	Off-Platform Light Trap CPUE (SE) Rank (%N)	Within-Platform Light Trap CPUE (SE) Rank (%N)	Surface Plankton Net Density (SE) Rank (%N)
Aulopiformes				
Chlorophthalmidae				
Unidentified (greeneyes)	Aug	0 (0)	0 (0)	0.03 (0.03) 75 (<1.0)
Synodontidae				
Saurida brasiliensis (largescale lizardfish)	Jun, Jul, Aug, Sep	0 (0)	0.16 (0.09) 8 (1.0)	1.18 (0.38) 23 (<1.0)
Synodus foetens (inshore lizardfish)	Jun, Jul, Sep	0.05 (0.04) 24 (<1.0)	0.90 (0.63) 3 (5.8)	0.01 (0.01) 86 (<1.0)
Trachinocephalus myops (snakefish)	Jun, Jul, Sep	0.07 (0.06) 19.5 (<1.0)	0.07 (0.04) 19.5 (<1.0)	0.04 (0.04) 71 (<1.0)
Paralepidae				
Lestrolepis intermedia (barracudina)	Jun	0 (0)	0 (0)	0.11 (0.09) 54 (<1.0)
Myctophiformes				
Myctophidae				
Unidentified (lanternfishes)	May, Jun, Aug, Sep	0.05 (0.05) 24 (<1.0)	0.06 (0.03) 21 (<1.0)	3.93 (1.45) 10 (<1.0)
Gadiformes				
Bregmacerotidae				
Bregmaceros cantori (codlet)	May, Jun, Jul, Sep	0.11 (0.06) 14 (1.2)	0.04 (0.02) 23.5 (<1.0)	3.58 (0.81) 11 (<1.0)
Ophidiiformes				
Ophidiidae				
Lepophidium staurophor (barred cusk-eel)	Jun, Jul, Aug	0 (0)	0 (0)	0.19 (0.09) 48 (<1.0)
Lophiiformes				
Caulophyrnidae				
Unidentified (anglerfishes)	Jun	0 (0)	0 (0)	0.02 (0.02) 84 (<1.0)
Ceratiidae				
Unidentified (seadevils)	Sep	0 (0)	0 (0)	0.06 (0.06) 68 (<1.0)
Atheriniformes				
Exocoetidae				
Unidentified (flyingfishes)	Jun, Jul, Sep	0.02 (0.02) 38 (<1.0)	0 (0)	0.47 (0.24) 33 (<1.0)
Atherinidae				
Membras martinica (rough silverside)	Jun	0 (0)	0.03 (0.03) 28 (<1.0)	0 (0)
Beryciformes				
Holocentridae (RA)				
Holocentrus spp. (squirrelfishes)	Jul, Sep	0.07 (0.03) 19.5 (<1.0)	0.13 (0.06) 12 (<1.0)	0 (0)

Table 2. Main Pass 259 (continued)

TAXA	Months Collected	Off-Platform Light Trap CPUE (SE) Rank (%N)	Within-Platform Light Trap CPUE (SE) Rank (%N)	Surface Plankton Net Density (SE) Rank (%N)
Scorpaeniformes				
Scorpaenidae				
Scorpaena spp. (scorpionfishes)	Jun, Jul, Aug, Sep	0 (0)	0 (0)	0.13 (0.07) 50 (<1.0)
Triglidae				
Prionotus spp. (searobins)	May	0 (0)	0 (0)	0.09 (0.06) 58 (<1.0)
Perciformes				
Unidentified	Jun, Jul, Aug, Sep	0.09 (0.09) 16.50 (<1.0)	0.01 (0.01) 36.5 (<1.0)	3.01 (1.07) 14 (<1.0)
Serranidae (RA)				
Anthinae (sea perches)	Jun, Sep	0 (0)	0 (0)	0.35 (0.16) 39 (<1.0)
Epinephelinae (groupers)	Jun, Jul, Aug	0.04 (0.04) 29.5 (<1.0)	0.03 (0.02) 28 (<1.0)	0.09 (0.07) 57 (<1.0)
Serraninae (sea basses)	Jun	0 (0)	0 (0)	0.11 (0.07) 52 (<1.0)
Priacanthidae				
Priacanthus spp. (bigeyes)	Jun	0 (0)	0 (0)	0.03 (0.03) 73.5 (<1.0)
Rachycentridae				
Rachycentron canadum (cobia)	Jun	0 (0)	0 (0)	0.02 (0.02) 82 (<1.0)
Echeneidae				
Unidentified (remoras)	Sep	0 (0)	0 (0)	0.07 (0.07) 65 (<1.0)
Carangidae				
Unidentified	Jul, Aug	0.02 (0.02) 38 (<1.0)	0.09 (0.06) 17.5 (<1.0)	6.51 (3.72) 7 (2.1)
Caranx spp.	Jun, Jul, Sep	0.02 (0.02) 38 (<1.0)	0 (0)	0.55 (0.35) 30 (<1.0)
Caranx crysos (blue runner)	May, Jun, Jul, Aug, Sep	0.18 (0.06) 9 (2.0)	0.16 (0.05) 8 (1.0)	7.17 (1.40) 6 (1.53)
Caranx hippos/latus (crevalle/horse-eye jack)	Jun, Aug	0 (0)	0.03 (0.02) 28 (<1.0)	0.02 (0.02) 82 (<1.0)
Chloroscombrus chrysurus (Atlantic bumper)	Jul, Aug, Sep	0.04 (0.03) 29.5 (<1.0)	0.04 (0.02) 23.5 (<1.0)	0.68 (0.39) 27 (<1.0)
Decapterus punctatus (round scad)	Jun, Jul, Aug	0.11 (0.07) 14 (1.2)	0.09 (0.04) 17.5 (<1.0)	0.42 (0.33) 36 (<1.0)
Elagatis bipinnulata (rainbow runner)	Jul	0 (0)	0 (0)	0.03 (0.03) 76 (<1.0)
Selar crumenophthalmus (bigeye scad)	Jul	0 (0)	0.01 (0.01) 36.5 (<1.0)	0.05 (0.05) 69 (<1.0)
Selene vomer (lookdown)	May, Jun	0 (0)	0 (0)	0.07 (0.05) 64 (<1.0)
Seriola spp. (amberjacks)	May, Jun, Jul	0 (0)	0 (0)	0.56 (0.31) 29 (<1.0)

Table 2. Main Pass 259 (continued)

TAXA	Months Collected	Off-Platform Light Trap CPUE (SE) Rank (%N)	Within-Platform Light Trap CPUE (SE) Rank (%N)	Surface Plankton Net Density (SE) Rank (%N)
Seriola zonata (banded rudderfish)	Jun	0.02 (0.02) 38 (<1.0)	0 (0)	0 (0)
Trachurus lathami (rough scad)	Aug	0 (0)	0 (0)	0.03 (0.03) 78 (<1.0)
Lutjanidae (RA)				
Unidentified	Jun	0.02 (0.02) 38 (<1.0)	0 (0)	0 (0)
Lutjanus campechanus (red snapper)	May	0 (0)	0 (0)	0.05 (0.05) 70 (<1.0)
Pristipomoides aquilonaris (wenchman)	May, Jun, Jul, Sep	0 (0)	0 (0)	0.31 (0.16) 42 (<1.0)
Rhomboplites aurorubens (vermilion snapper)	Jun	0 (0)	0 (0)	0.03 (0.03) 77 (<1.0)
Sparidae				
Lagodon rhomboides (pinfish)	Jun	0 (0)	0 (0)	0.02 (0.02) 79 (<1.0)
Sciaenidae				
Cynoscion arenarius (sand seatrout)	Jul	0 (0)	0 (0)	0.46 (0.27) 34 (<1.0)
Menticirrhus spp. (kingfish)	Aug	0 (0)	0 (0)	0.07 (0.05) 62 (<1.0)
Pomacentridae (RD)				
Pomacentrus spp. (damselfishes)	Jul	0.07 (0.06) 19.5 (<1.0)	0.04 (0.03) 23.5 (<1.0)	0 (0)
Mugilidae				
Mugil curema (white mullet)	May, Jun	0 (0)	0 (0)	0.15 (0.09) 49 (<1.0)
Sphyraenidae				
Sphyraena spp.	May, Jun	0 (0)	0 (0)	0.28 (0.16) 44 (<1.0)
Sphyraena barracuda (great barracuda)	Sep	0 (0)	0 (0)	0.06 (0.06) 66 (<1.0)
Sphyraena guachancho (guaguanche)	May, Jun, Jul	0 (0)	0 (0)	0.36 (0.18) 38 (<1.0)
Labridae (RD)				
Unidentified	Jun, Aug, Sep	0 (0)	0 (0)	0.34 (0.14) 40 (<1.0)
Thalassoma spp. (wrasses)	Jun	0 (0)	0 (0)	0.07 (0.07) 63 (<1.0)
Scaridae (RD)				
Unidentified (parrotfishes)	Aug	0 (0)	0 (0)	0.11 (0.08) 55 (<1.0)

Table 2. Main Pass 259 (continued)

TAXA	Months Collected	Off-Platform Light Trap CPUE (SE) Rank (%N)	Within-Platform Light Trap CPUE (SE) Rank (%N)	Surface Plankton Net Density (SE) Rank (%N)
Blenniidae (RA)				
Unidentified	May, Jun, Jul, Aug, Sep	0 (0)	0.02 (0.02) 30.5 (<1.0)	2.06 (0.54) 18 (<1.0)
Hypsoblennius invemar (tesselated blenny)	Jul	0.38 (0.22) 5 (4.2)	0.03 (0.02) 28 (<1.0)	0 (0)
Scartella cristata (molly miller)	Jul	0 (0)	0 (0)	0.02 (0.02) 85 (<1.0)
Callionymidae				
Callionymus pauciradiatus (spotted dragonet)	Aug	0 (0)	0 (0)	0.08 (0.06) 60 (<1.0)
Gobiidae				
Unidentified	May, Jun, Jul, Aug, Sep	0.09 (0.04) 16.5 (1.0)	0.03 (0.02) 28 (<1.0)	10.46 (1.51) 5 (1.63)
Gobiosoma bosc (naked goby)	May, Jun	0 (0)	0 (0)	0.95 (0.57) 24 (<1.0)
Microdesmidae				
Microdesmus spp.	May, Jun, Jul, Aug	0.02 (0.02) 38 (<1.0)	0.01 (0.01) 36.5 (<1.0)	0.54 (0.26) 32 (<1.0)
Microdesmus lanceolatus (lancetail wormfish)	May, Jun, Jul, Aug, Sep	0.04 (0.03) 29.5 (<1.0)	0 (0)	1.28 (0.32) 22 (<1.0)
Trichiuridae				
Trichiurus lepturus (Atlantic cutlassfish)	May, Jun, Jul, Sep	0.02 (0.02) 38 (<1.0)	0.01 (0.01) 36.5 (<1.0)	0.40 (0.17) 37 (<1.0)
Scombridae				
Unidentified	May, Jun, Jul	0.02 (0.02) 38 (<1.0)	0.01 (0.01) 36.5 (<1.0)	0.26 (0.19) 47 (<1.0)
Auxis spp. (frigate mackerels)	May, Jun, Jul, Aug, Sep	0.13 (0.06) 11.5 (1.4)	0.19 (0.07) 6 (1.5)	5.77 (2.14) 8 (2.2)
Euthynnus alletteratus (little tunny)	Jun, Jul, Aug, Sep	0.29 (0.11) 6 (3.2)	0.10 (0.04) 14.5 (<1.0)	3.19 (1.12) 13 (<1.0)
Katsuwonus pelamis (skipjack tuna)	Jul	0.05 (0.05) 24 (<1.0)	0 (0)	0 (0)
Scomberomorus cavalla (king mackerel)	May, Jun, Jul, Aug	0.04 (0.03) 29.5 (<1.0)	0.01 (0.01) 36.5 (<1.0)	0.57 (0.17) 28 (<1.0)
Scomberomorus maculatus (Spanish mackerel)	May, Jun, Jul, Aug	0.05 (0.03) 24 (<1.0)	0.01 (0.01) 36.5 (<1.0)	0.70 (0.27) 26 (<1.0)
Thunnus spp. (tunas)	Jun, Sep	0.13 (0.07) 11.5 (1.4)	0.09 (0.05) 16 (<1.0)	0.33 (0.17) 41 (<1.0)
Stromatoideae				
Unidentified	Jun, Jul, Aug, Sep	0.05 (0.03) 24 (<1.0)	0 (0)	1.69 (0.66) 20 (<1.0)
Ariommidae				
Ariomma spp. (driftfish)	May, Jul	0 (0)	0 (0)	0.08 (0.06) 61 (<1.0)

Table 2. Main Pass 259 (continued)

TAXA	Months Collected	Off-Platform Light Trap CPUE (SE) Rank (%N)	Within-Platform Light Trap CPUE (SE) Rank (%N)	Surface Plankton Net Density (SE) Rank (%N)
Nomeidae				
Unidentified	Sep	0 (0)	0 (0)	0.12 (0.12) 51 (<1.0)
Psenes spp. (driftfish)	Jun	0 (0)	0 (0)	0.02 (0.02) 82 (<1.0)
Cubiceps pauciradiatus (bigeye cigarfish)	Jun, Jul, Sep	0 (0)	0 (0)	0.82 (0.39) 25 (<1.0)
Pleuronectiformes				
Bothidae				
Bothus spp. (eyed/spottail flounder)	Jun, Aug, Sep	0 (0)	0 (0)	1.47 (0.42) 21 (<1.0)
Citharichthys spp. (whiffs)	Jun, Jul, Aug	0 (0)	0 (0)	0.28 (0.17) 46 (<1.0)
Etropus crossotus (fringed flounder)	Jun, Jul, Aug	0 (0)	0 (0)	0.55 (0.25) 31 (<1.0)
Syacium spp. (dusky/shoal flounder)	May, Jun, Jul, Aug	0.02 (0.02) 38 (<1.0)	0.01 (0.01) 36.5 (<1.0)	0.43 (0.19) 35 (<1.0)
Cynoglossidae				
Symphurus spp. (tonguefish)	Jun, Jul, Aug, Sep	0.04 (0.04) 29.5 (<1.0)	0.02 (0.02) 30.5 (<1.0)	2.20 (0.49) 17 (<1.0)
Tetraodontiformes				
Balistidae				
Unidentified	Jun, Jul	0 (0)	0 (0)	0.28 (0.19) 45 (<1.0)
Monacanthus spp. (filefish)	Jun	0 (0)	0 (0)	0.03 (0.03) 72 (<1.0)
Monacanthus hispidus (planehead filefish)	Jun	0 (0)	0 (0)	0.03 (0.03) 73.5 (<1.0)

18

Table 3. Mean light trap CPUE (fish/10 min) and plankton net density (fish/100 m^3) for fish collected at Viosca Knoll 203, with standard error (SE), rank based on CPUE or densities, and percent of total catch (%N). For ranks, tied values received the mean of the corresponding ranks. RA = reef associated, RD = reef dependent.

TAXA	Months Collected	Off-Platform Light Trap CPUE (SE) Rank (%N)	Within-Platform Light Trap CPUE (SE) Rank (%N)	Surface Plankton Net Density (SE) Rank (%N)
Anguilliformes				
Muraenidae				
Unidentified (moray eels)	Jun, Oct	0 (0)	0.03 (0.03) 40.5 (<1.0)	0.15 (0.11) 68 (<1.0)
Ophichthidae				
Ophichthus spp. (snake eels)	May, Jun, Jul, Aug	0.05 (0.03) 27.5 (<1.0)	0.32 (0.09) 16 (1.5)	3.13 (0.93) 15 (1.5)
Ophichthus gomesi (shrimp eel)	May, Jun, Jul	0.02 (0.02) 49.5 (<1.0)	0.12 (0.05) 27.5 (<1.0)	0.36 (0.28) 44 (<1.0)
Clupeiformes				
Clupeidae				
Harengula jaguana (scaled sardine)	May, Jun, Jul, Aug	1.97 (0.89) 2 (15.9)	2.05 (0.59) 3 (9.8)	23.69 (6.61) 4 (6.8)
Opisthonema oglinum (Atlantic thread herring)	May, Jun, Jul, Aug	0.08 (0.04) 22 (<1.0)	1.27 (0.65) 6 (6.1)	12.17 (3.83) 10 (4.2)
Sardinella aurita (Spanish sardine)	May, Jun, Jul	0.02 (0.02) 49.5 (<1.0)	0.07 (0.03) 35.5 (<1.0)	0.05 (0.05) 85 (<1.0)
Engraulidae				
Unidentified	May, Jun, Jul, Oct	0.04 (0.03) 31.5 (<1.0)	0.13 (0.06) 26 (<1.0)	16.89 (7.57) 6 (4.8)
Anchoa spp.	May, Jun, Jul, Aug, Oct	1.22 (0.32) 3 (9.9)	0.53 (0.21) 11 (2.5)	179.50 (75.10) 1 (26.1)
Anchoa hepsetus (striped herring)	May, Jun, Jul, Aug, Oct	0.05 (0.03) 27.5 (<1.0)	0.83 (0.24) 8 (4.0)	15.85 (5.94) 7 (3.4)
Anchoa mitchilli (bay anchovy)	Jun, Jul, Aug	0.02 (0.02) 49.5 (<1.0)	0.02 (0.02) 53.5 (<1.0)	0.09 (0.07) 79 (<1.0)
Anchoa nasuta (longnose anchovy)	May, Jun, Jul	0.02 (0.02) 49.5 (<1.0)	0.10 (0.05) 29 (<1.0)	0.63 (0.50) 33 (<1.0)
Anchoa nasuta/hepsetus (longnose/striped anchovy)	Jun, Jul, Aug	0 (0)	0 (0)	36.28 (13.57) 3 (12.9)
Anchoviella perfasciata (flat anchovy)	Jun, Jul	0 (0)	0.27 (0.19) 17 (1.3)	0 (0)
Engraulis eurystole (silver anchovy)	May, Jun, Jul, Aug, Oct	0.17 (0.09) 13.5 (1.3)	1.80 (0.38) 4 (8.6)	12.97 (6.45) 9 (1.5)
Stomiiformes				
Gonostomatidae				
Cyclothone spp. (bristlemouths)	Jun	0 (0)	0 (0)	0.12 (0.12) 74 (<1.0)
Aulopiformes				
Synodontidae				
Saurida brasiliensis (largescale lizardfish)	May, Jun, Jul, Aug, Oct	0.36 (0.10) 9 (2.9)	2.57 (1.66) 1.5 (12.3)	2.68 (0.84) 16 (1.0)
Synodus foetens (inshore lizardfish)	May, Jun, Jul, Aug, Oct	0.03 (0.03) 35 (<1.0)	2.57 (0.91) 1.5 (12.3)	0.23 (0.17) 57 (<1.0)

19

Table 3. Viosca Knoll 203 (continued)

TAXA	Months Collected	Off-Platform Light Trap CPUE (SE) Rank (%N)	Within-Platform Light Trap CPUE (SE) Rank (%N)	Surface Plankton Net Density (SE) Rank (%N)
Synodus poeyi (offshore lizardfish)	Jun	0 (0)	0.02 (0.02) 53.5 (<1.0)	0 (0)
Trachinocephalus myops (snakefish)	May, Jun, Aug	0.02 (0.02) 49.5 (<1.0)	0.02 (0.02) 53.5 (<1.0)	0.06 (0.04) 84 (<1.0)
Myctophiformes				
Myctophidae				
Unidentified (lanternfishes)	May, Jun, Jul	0.07 (0.03) 23.5 (<1.0)	0 (0)	0.33 (0.15) 47 (<1.0)
Gadiformes				
Bregmacerotidae				
Bregmaceros cantori (codlet)	May, Jun, Jul, Aug, Oct	0.39 (0.16) 8 (3.2)	0.20 (0.09) 24 (<1.0)	14.21 (4.68) 8 (7.9)
Ophidiiformes				
Ophidiidae				
Lepophidium staurophor (barred cusk-eel)	May, Jun, Oct	0.02 (0.02) 49.5 (<1.0)	0 (0)	0.27 (0.17) 52 (<1.0)
Ophidion spp. (cusk-eels)	Jun, Jul, Oct	0.02 (0.02) 49.5 (<1.0)	0 (0)	0.35 (0.29) 46 (<1.0)
Ophidion nocomis (cusk-eels)	May, Jun, Jul, Oct	0.02 (0.02) 49.5 (<1.0)	0.05 (0.03) 38.5 (<1.0)	1.65 (0.51) 22 (<1.0)
Atheriniformes				
Atherinidae				
Membras martinica (rough silverside)	Jun	0 (0)	0.02 (0.02) 53.5 (<1.0)	0 (0)
Scorpaeniformes				
Scorpaenidae				
Scorpaena spp. (scorpionfishes)	May, Jun, Oct	0.02 (0.02) 49.5 (<1.0)	0.08 (0.05) 31.5 (<1.0)	0.62 (0.24) 34 (<1.0)
Triglidae				
Prionotus spp. (searobins)	May	0 (0)	0 (0)	0.08 (0.08) 81 (<1.0)
Perciformes				
Unidentified	May, Jun, Jul, Aug, Oct	0.04 (0.03) 31.5 (<1.0)	0 (0)	3.48 (0.89) 13 (1.1)
Serranidae (RA)				
Anthinae (sea perches)	Jun	0.02 (0.02) 49.5 (<1.0)	0 (0)	0.10 (0.10) 77 (<1.0)
Epinephelinae (groupers)	Jul	0 (0)	0 (0)	0.04 (0.04) 87 (<1.0)
Grammistinae (basslets)	May, Jun	0 (0)	0.02 (0.02) 53.5 (<1.0)	0.16 (0.13) 67 (<1.0)
Serraninae (sea basses)	May, Jun, Jul, Oct	0.02 (0.02) 49.5 (<1.0)	0.02 (0.02) 53.5 (<1.0)	0.81 (0.30) 29 (<1.0)
Apogonidae				
Unidentified (cardinalfishes)	May, Jun	0 (0)	0.02 (0.02) 53.5 (<1.0)	0.10 (0.10) 78 (<1.0)

Table 3. Viosca Knoll 203 (continued)

TAXA	Months Collected	Off-Platform Light Trap CPUE (SE) Rank (%N)	Within-Platform Light Trap CPUE (SE) Rank (%N)	Surface Plankton Net Density (SE) Rank (%N)
Rachycentridae				
Rachycentron canadum (cobia)	Jun	0 (0)	0 (0)	0.21 (0.16) 60 (<1.0)
Carangidae				
Unidentified	Jul, Oct	0 (0)	0 (0)	0.18 (0.13) 62 (<1.0)
Caranx spp	Jun, Jul, Aug	0 (0)	0.02 (0.02) 53.5 (<1.0)	1.07 (0.48) 24 (<1.0)
Caranx crysos (blue runner)	May, Jun, Jul, Oct	0.17 (0.10) 13.5 (1.3)	0.43 (0.21) 13 (2.1)	2.19 (0.75) 19 (<1.0)
Caranx latus (horse-eye jack)	Jun	0 (0)	0.02 (0.02) 53.5 (<1.0)	0 (0)
Chloroscombrus chrysurus (Atlantic bumper)	May, Jun, Jul, Aug, Oct	0.03 (0.02) 35 (<1.0)	0.07 (0.03) 35.5 (<1.0)	2.24 (0.77) 18 (<1.0)
Decapterus punctatus (round scad)	May, Jun, Jul, Aug, Oct	0.69 (0.22) 5 (5.5)	1.28 (0.39) 5 (6.1)	0.48 (0.27) 38 (<1.0)
Seriola spp. (amberjacks)	May, Jun, Jul	0.02 (0.02) 49.5 (<1.0)	0 (0)	0.91 (0.46) 26 (<1.0)
Seriola zonata (banded rudderfish)	May	0 (0)	0.02 (0.02) 53.5 (<1.0)	0.13 (0.13) 72.5 (<1.0)
Trachurus lathami (rough scad)	May	0 (0)	0.02 (0.02) 53.5 (<1.0)	0 (0)
Lutjanidae (RA)				
Lutjanus spp.	May, Jun, Jul, Aug	0.05 (0.03) 27.5 (<1.0)	0.02 (0.02) 53.5 (<1.0)	0.99 (0.50) 25 (<1.0)
Lutjanus campechanus (red snapper)	May, Jun, Jul	0.01 (0.01) 62.5 (<1.0)	0.23 (0.15) 20 (1.1)	0.28 (0.21) 50 (<1.0)
Lutjanus griseus (gray snapper)	Aug	0.33 (0.21) 10 (2.7)	0.02 (0.02) 53.5 (<1.0)	0.26 (0.26) 53.5 (<1.0)
Lutjanus synagris (lane snapper)	Jul	0 (0)	0 (0)	0.11 (0.08) 75 (<1.0)
Ocyurus chrysurus (yellowtail snapper)	Jun	0 (0)	0.03 (0.02) 53.5 (<1.0)	0 (0)
Rhomboplites aurorubens (vermilion snapper)	Jul, Aug, Oct	0.16 (0.05) 15 (1.2)	0.08 (0.04) 31.5 (<1.0)	0.18 (0.18) 63 (<1.0)
Gerreidae				
Unidentified	May, Jun	0.07 (0.05) 23.5 (<1.0)	0.04 (0.02) 53.5 (<1.0)	0.42 (0.23) 40 (<1.0)
Eucinostomus spp. (mojarras)	Jun, Jul, Aug, Oct	0.10 (0.05) 18.5 (<1.0)	0.58 (0.26) 10 (2.8)	0.66 (0.40) 32 (<1.0)
Sparidae				
Unidentified	Jun, Jul, Aug	0 (0)	0 (0)	0.68 (0.38) 31 (<1.0)
Lagodon rhomboides (pinfish)	Jun	0 (0)	0 (0)	0.14 (0.14) 70 (<1.0)

Table 3. Viosca Knoll 203 (continued)

TAXA	Months Collected	Off-Platform Light Trap CPUE (SE) Rank (%N)	Within-Platform Light Trap CPUE (SE) Rank (%N)	Surface Plankton Net Density (SE) Rank (%N)
Sciaenidae				
Cynoscion arenarius (sand seatrout)	May, Jun, Jul, Aug, Oct	0.02 (0.02) 49.5 (<1.0)	0.05 (0.02) 53.5 (<1.0)	7.92 (2.44) 11 (1.4)
Cynoscion nothus (silver seatrout)	May, Jun	0.02 (0.02) 49.5 (<1.0)	0.06 (0.02) 53.5 (<1.0)	0.45 (0.22) 39 (<1.0)
Menticirrhus spp. (kingfish)	May, Jun	0.02 (0.02) 49.5 (<1.0)	0 (0)	0.24 (0.15) 56 (<1.0)
Micropogonias undulatus (Atlantic croaker)	Oct	0.10 (0.06) 20 (<1.0)	0.12 (0.06) 27.5 (<1.0)	20.39 (9.94) 5 (4.7)
Sciaenops ocellatus (red drum)	Oct	0 (0)	0 (0)	0.09 (0.09) 80 (<1.0)
Mullidae				
Unidentified (goatfishes)	May	0 (0)	0.07 (0.07) 35.5 (<1.0)	0 (0)
Ephippidae				
Chaetodipterus faber (Atlantic spadefish)	May	0.02 (0.02) 49.5 (<1.0)	0 (0)	0 (0)
Pomacentridae (RD)				
Pomacentrus spp. (damselfishes)	Jun, Jul, Aug	0.51 (0.15) 6 (4.1)	0.35 (0.10) 15 (1.7)	0 (0)
Mugilidae				
Mugil cephalus (striped mullet)	May	0.02 (0.02) 49.5 (<1.0)	0 (0)	0 (0)
Mugil curema (white mullet)	May	0 (0)	0.02 (0.02) 53.5 (<1.0)	0 (0)
Sphyraenidae				
Sphyraena spp.	May, Jun, Jul	0 (0)	0 (0)	0.59 (0.27) 36 (<1.0)
Sphyraena borealis (northern sennet)	Jun, Jul	0.05 (0.04) 27.5 (<1.0)	0 (0)	2.27 (0.89) 17 (<1.0)
Sphyraena guachancho (guaguanche)	Jun	0 (0)	0.08 (0.05) 31.5 (<1.0)	0 (0)
Opisthognathidae				
Opisthognathus spp. (jawfishes)	May, Jun	0.02 (0.02) 49.5 (<1.0)	0 (0)	0.21 (0.18) 59 (<1.0)
Blenniidae (RA)				
Unidentified	May, Jun, Jul, Aug	0.01 (0.01) 62.5 (<1.0)	0.02 (0.02) 53.5 (<1.0)	0.61 (0.24) 35 (<1.0)
Chasmodes spp. (Florida/striped blenny)	Jun, Jul, Aug	0 (0)	0.03 (0.03) 40.5 (<1.0)	0.50 (0.31) 37 (<1.0)
Hypleurochilus multifilis (blenny)	May, Jun	0 (0)	0.22 (0.11) 23 (1.0)	0.14 (0.14) 69 (<1.0)
Hypsoblennius hentzi (feather blenny)	May, Jun	0 (0)	0.07 (0.04) 35.5 (<1.0)	0 (0)
Hypsoblennius invemar (tesselated blenny)	May, Jun, Jul, Aug	2.46 (0.81) 1 (19.7)	0.23 (0.07) 20 (1.1)	0 (0)

Table 3. Viosca Knoll 203 (continued)

TAXA	Months Collected	Off-Platform Light Trap CPUE (SE) Rank (%N)	Within-Platform Light Trap CPUE (SE) Rank (%N)	Surface Plankton Net Density (SE) Rank (%N)
Hypsoblennius ionthas (freckled blenny)	Jun, Jul, Aug	0.12 (0.09) 17 (<1.0)	0.23 (0.11) 20 (1.1)	0.05 (0.05) 86 (<1.0)
Ophioblennius macclurei (redlip blenny)	May, Jun	0 (0)	0 (0)	0.30 (0.22) 49 (<1.0)
Parablennius marmoreus (seaweed blenny)	May, Jun, Jul, Aug	0.10 (0.07) 18.5 (<1.0)	0.45 (0.11) 12 (2.1)	0 (0)
Scartella cristata (molly miller)	May, Jun, Jul, Aug	0.25 (0.09) 12 (2.0)	0.17 (0.08) 25 (<1.0)	3.15 (1.01) 14 (<1.0)
Callionymidae				
Unidentified (dragonets)	Oct	0 (0)	0 (0)	0.37 (0.28) 43 (<1.0)
Gobiidae				
Unidentified	May, Jun, Jul, Aug, Oct	0.29 (0.07) 11 (2.5)	0.23 (0.09) 20 (1.1)	44.72 (10.15) 2 (11.8)
Gobionellus oceanicus (sharptail goby)	Jun	0 (0)	0 (0)	0.10 (0.10) 76 (<1.0)
Gobiosoma bosc (naked goby)	Jun	0.03 (0.03) 35 (<1.0)	0 (0)	0.39 (0.39) 42 (<1.0)
Microgobius sp. (clown/green goby)	May	0 (0)	0 (0)	0.26 (0.26) 53.5 (<1.0)
Microdesmidae				
Microdesmus spp.	May, Jul	0 (0)	0 (0)	0.33 (0.17) 48 (<1.0)
Microdesmus lanceolatus (lancetail wormfish)	May, Jun, Jul	0.02 (0.02) 49.5 (<1.0)	0.03 (0.02) 53.5 (<1.0)	3.64 (0.81) 12 (<1.0)
Microdesmus longipinnis (pink wormfish)	May, Jun	0.02 (0.02) 49.5 (<1.0)	0 (0)	0.19 (0.10) 61 (<1.0)
Trichiuridae				
Trichiurus lepturus (Atlantic cutlassfish)	Jul, Aug	0 (0)	0 (0)	0.17 (0.15) 65 (<1.0)
Scombridae				
Auxis spp. (frigate mackerels)	May, Jun, Jul, Oct	1.19 (0.43) 4 (9.7)	0.67 (0.24) 9 (3.2)	0.36 (0.28) 45 (<1.0)
Euthynnus alletteratus (little tunny)	May, Jun, Jul, Aug	0.40 (0.15) 7 (3.2)	1.17 (0.48) 7 (5.6)	0.85 (0.41) 27 (<1.0)
Scomberomorus cavalla (king mackerel)	May, Jun, Jul, Aug	0.05 (0.03) 27.5 (<1.0)	0.23 (0.09) 20 (1.1)	0.17 (0.13) 64 (<1.0)
Scomberomorus maculatus (Spanish mackerel)	May, Jun, Jul, Aug	0.14 (0.05) 16 (1.2)	0.42 (0.18) 14 (2.0)	1.85 (1.01) 21 (<1.0)
Thunnus spp. (tunas)	Jun, Aug	0.02 (0.02) 49.5 (<1.0)	0.05 (0.03) 38.5 (<1.0)	0.84 (0.61) 28 (<1.0)
Thunnus thynnus (bluefin tuna)	May, Jun	0.08 (0.04) 21 (<1.0)	0 (0)	0 (0)
Ariommidae				
Ariomma spp. (driftfish)	Jun	0.02 (0.02) 49.5 (<1.0)	0.04 (0.02) 53.5 (<1.0)	0.07 (0.05) 82.5 (<1.0)

Table 3. Viosca Knoll 203 (continued)

TAXA	Months Collected	Off-Platform Light Trap CPUE (SE) Rank (%N)	Within-Platform Light Trap CPUE (SE) Rank (%N)	Surface Plankton Net Density (SE) Rank (%N)
Stromateidae				
Peprilus burti (gulf butterfish)	Oct	0 (0)	0 (0)	0.13 (0.13) 72.5 (<1.0)
Peprilus paru (harvestfish)	May, Aug	0.03 (0.02) 35 (<1.0)	0 (0)	0.78 (0.78) 30 (<1.0)
Pleuronectiformes				
Bothidae				
Bothus spp. (eyed/spottail flounder)	Jun	0 (0)	0 (0)	0.07 (0.05) 82.5 (<1.0)
Etropus crossotus (fringed flounder)	May, Jun, Jul, Aug	0.05 (0.03) 27.5 (<1.0)	0 (0)	1.24 (0.56) 23 (<1.0)
Syacium spp. (dusky/shoal flounder)	May, Jun, Jul, Oct	0.02 (0.02) 49.5 (<1.0)	0.08 (0.04) 31.5 (<1.0)	0.41 (0.19) 41 (<1.0)
Cynoglossidae				
Symphurus spp. (tonguefish)	May, Jun, Jul, Aug	0.02 (0.02) 49.5 (<1.0)	0.02 (0.02) 53.5 (<1.0)	1.87 (0.58) 20 (<1.0)
Tetraodontiformes				
Balistidae				
Monacanthus spp. (filefish)	May, Jul	0.03 (0.02) 35 (<1.0)	0 (0)	0.21 (0.21) 58 (<1.0)
Tetraodontidae				
Sphoeroides spp. (pufferfish)	Aug	0 (0)	0 (0)	0.03 (0.03) 89 (<1.0)
Sphoeroides parvus (least puffer)	Jul	0 (0)	0 (0)	0.17 (0.17) 66 (<1.0)

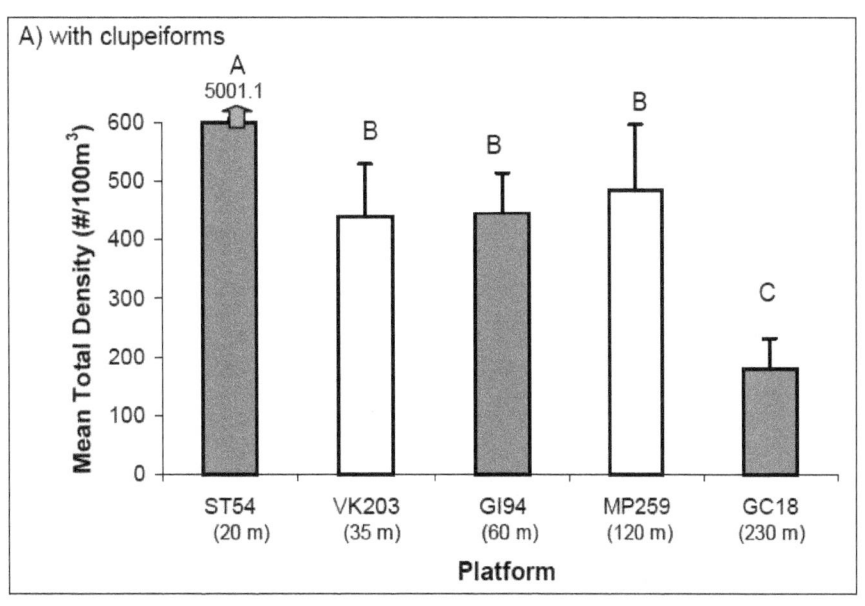

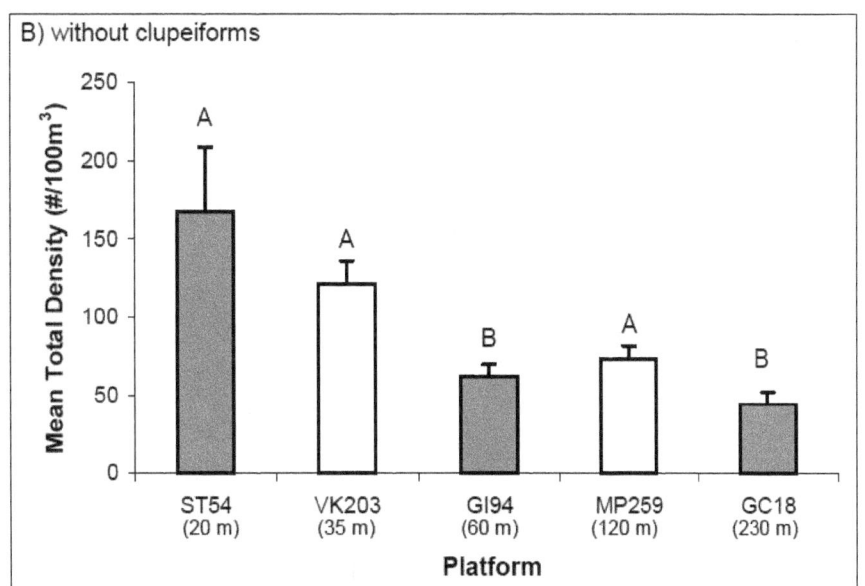

Figure 4. Mean total densities of fishes from plankton nets (with standard errors) at each platform for data a) with clupeiforms and b) without clupeiforms. Different letters above bars indicate significant differences between platform densities using Tukey's Studentized Range Test. Open bars represent platforms east of the Delta. Numbers in parentheses indicates the depth, in meters, of each platform.

25

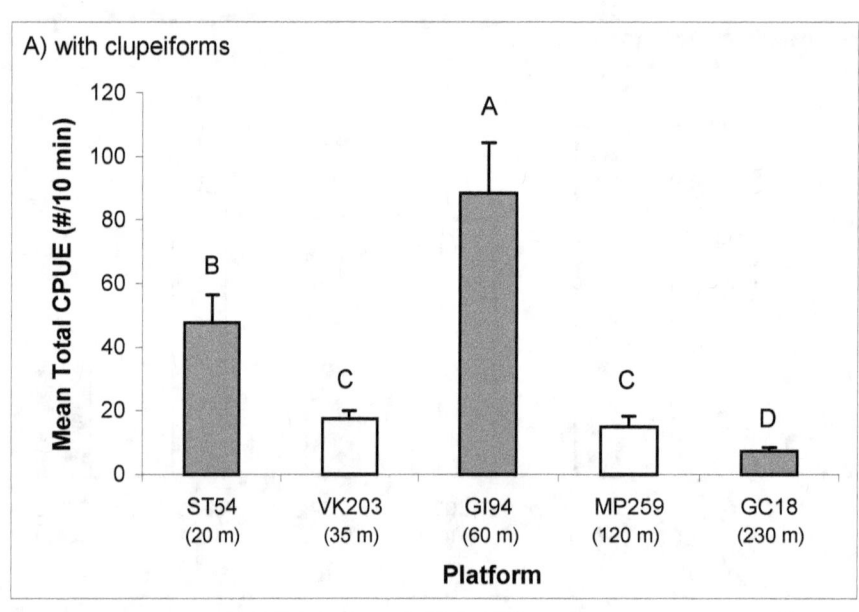

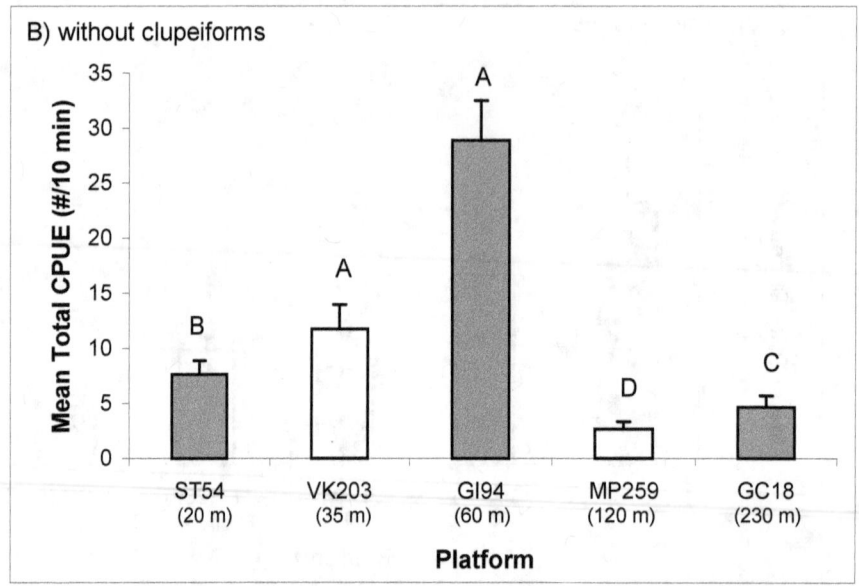

Figure 5. Mean total CPUEs of fishes from light traps (with standard errors) at each platform for data a) with clupeiforms and b) without clupeiforms. Different letters above bars indicate significant differences between platform CPUEs using Tukey's Studentized Range Test. Open bars represent platforms East of the Delta. Numbers in parentheses indicate the depth, in meters, of each platform.

Mean CPUEs from light traps were generally highest at platforms of intermediate depth (Figure 5). With clupeiforms included, mean CPUEs were significantly different between platforms (χ^2 = 158.85, p<0.0001), with highest catches at mid-shelf (GI 94 = 88.5 fish/10 min. ± 15.8) and lowest at the outer shelf (GC 18 = 7.2 ± 1.2; Figure 5a). The inner shelf platform ST 54 had the second highest mean CPUE (47.7 ± 8.7), due to high abundances of *Opisthonema oglinum*. With clupeiforms excluded, mean CPUEs were significantly different (χ^2 = 118.37, p<0.0001), with highest catches at the mid-shelf platforms, GI 94 and VK 203 (Figure 5b).

Taxonomic richness and diversity were also highest, for both gear types, at platforms of intermediate depth (35-120 m depth; Table 4). The number of taxa (identified to at least the genus level) and families collected, for both plankton nets and light traps, peaked at the mid-shelf platform GI 94, and were generally lowest at the two depth extremes. Light trap collections at the outer shelf platform MP 259, however, appeared to have exceptionally low taxonomic richness, and this may be manifested in its low diversity value. The higher number of taxa and families at GI 94 may be the result of the higher number of samples taken at this platform. Mean Shannon-Wiener diversity indices, which accounted for unequal sample sizes, showed a similar pattern of greatest diversity at intermediate depths. Plankton net diversity was significantly higher for the outer shelf platform MP 259 (χ^2 = 28.50, p<0.0001). Light trap diversity was significantly higher for the mid-shelf platforms VK 203 and GI 94 (χ^2 = 66.01, p<0.0001).

Numerical classification of the non-clupeiform larval and juvenile fish assemblages collected at each platform indicated that highest similarity occurred between platforms of similar depth (Figure 6). Although similarity was low for each platform pairing (mean similarity index = 0.371 ± 0.03) three groups were described. The most similar pair was the two outer shelf platforms, GC 18 and MP 259. Larval and juvenile fish assemblages at these platforms were characterized by relatively high numbers of *Auxis* spp. (10.2% and 19.1% of the total non-clupeiform catch, respectively) and *Caranx crysos* (6.6% and 13.3%), and included taxa such as *Holocentrus* spp. and unidentified myctophids and scarids (Table 5). The next most similar group consisted of the mid-shelf platforms, GI 94 and VK 203. High numbers of *Bregmaceros cantori* (6.5% and 13.5%, respectively), *Hypsoblennius invemar* (15.1% and 6.0%) and *Saurida brasiliensis* (9.6% and 8.0%) occurred at these platforms. The mid-shelf platforms also had the highest numbers of reef taxa, particularly blenniids, pomacentrids and lutjanids. The third group consisted of the inner shelf platform ST 54. This platform was dominated by *Cynoscion arenarius* (30.3%) and *Synodus foetens* (20.5%), and included other coastal taxa such as *Scomberomorus maculatus* and the blenniid complex *Scartella/Hypleurochilus*.

Several taxa were more abundant at platforms either east or west of the Delta, regardless of the sampling gear used (Table 6). *Decapterus punctatus*, *Eucinostomus* spp., *Lutjanus* spp., and Ophichthidae were significantly more abundant east of the Delta in both plankton nets and light traps. *Microdesmus lanceolatus* was significantly more abundant east of the Delta only in plankton nets, while *Thunnus* spp. was significantly more abundant east of the Delta only in light traps. *Caranx hippos/latus* was the only taxa significantly more abundant west of the Delta in both gear types. *Cynoscion arenarius*, *Euthynnus alletteratus*, *Peprilus burti*, *Scomberomorus cavalla*, and *Symphurus* spp. were significantly more abundant west of the Delta in light traps.

Table 4. Taxonomic richness and mean Shannon-Weiner Diversity (with standard errors) for the larval and juvenile fish assemblages collected at each platform. Different letters beside diversity values indicate significant differences between indices using the Tukey's Studentized Range Test. Numbers in parentheses indicate depth, in meters, of each platform. n = number of samples for a gear type. ‡ denotes platforms east of the Delta.

Plankton Net	n	Families	Taxa	Diversity
GC18 (230 m)	47	38	54	0.726 ± 0.094 (C)
MP259 (120 m) ‡	54	38	60	1.347 ± 0.085 (A)
GI94 (60 m)	144	40	73	0.929 ± 0.054 (B/C)
VK203 (35 m) ‡	56	32	65	1.181 ± 0.081 (A/B)
ST54 (20 m)	65	26	44	0.856 ± 0.081 (C)

Light Trap	n	Families	Taxa	Diversity
GC18 (230 m)	96	31	48	0.761 ± 0.061 (B)
MP259 (120 m) ‡	94	20	35	0.826 ± 0.064 (B)
GI94 (60 m)	267	37	80	1.105 ± 0.033 (A)
VK203 (35 m) ‡	112	31	67	1.267 ± 0.053 (A)
ST54 (20 m)	122	31	55	0.887 ± 0.052 (B)

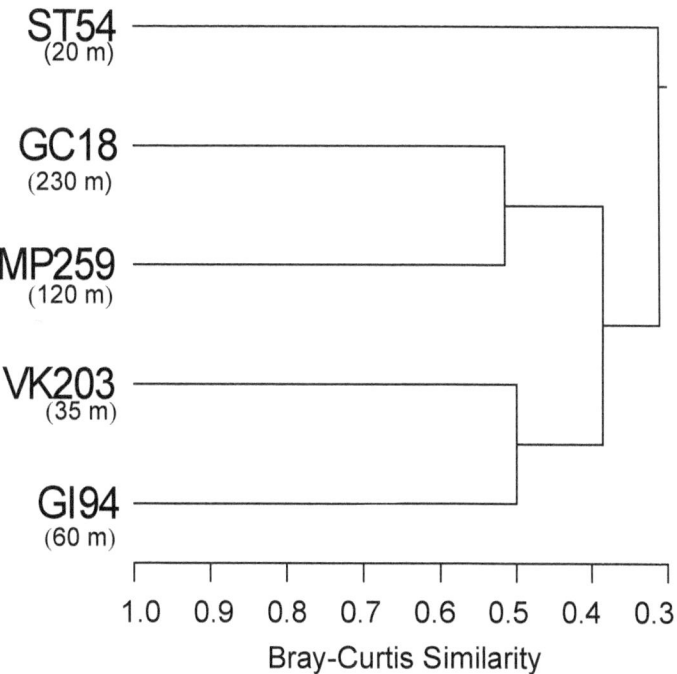

Figure 6. Cluster diagram of the overall larval and juvenile fish assemblages, with clupeiforms excluded, collected from all gears combined at each platform. Numbers in parentheses indicate the depth, in meters, of each platform. Samples were clustered using group-average sorting and the Bray-Curtis similarity index.

Table 5. Relative abundance (% of total catch from plankton nets and light traps combined) of the ten most abundant non-clupeiform taxa, and reef taxa that comprised >0.5%, at each platform. Numbers in parentheses indicate the depth, in meters, of each platform. RA = reef associated, RD = reef dependent.

ST 54 (20 m) - inner shelf

			%
Dominant	*Cynoscion arenarius*		30.3
Taxa	*Synodus foetens*		20.5
	Gobiidae		5.4
	Scomberomorus maculatus		4.9
	Euthynnus alletteratus		4.1
	Scartella/Hypleurochilus	RA	3.0
	Scomberomorus cavalla		2.6
	Caranx hippos/latus		2.4
	Hypsoblennius hentz/ionthas	RA	2.4
	Hypsoblennius invemar	RA	2.0

GI 94 (60 m) - mid-shelf

			%
Dominant	*Synodus poeyi*		15.3
Taxa	*Hypsoblennius invemar*	RA	15.1
	Parablennius marmoreus	RA	11.2
	Saurida brasiliensis		9.6
	Euthynnus alletteratus		8.0
	Bregmaceros cantori		6.5
	Symphurus spp.		4.9
	Synodus foetens		4.2
	Gobiidae		3.8
	Auxis spp.		3.4
Reef Taxa	*Hypsoblennius hentz/ionthas*	RA	2.8
	Scartella/Hypleurochilus	RA	1.8
	Pomacentrus spp.	RD	0.8
	Chromis spp.	RD	0.8
	Rhomboplites aurorubens	RA	0.5

VK 203 (35 m) - mid-shelf

			%
Dominant	Gobiidae		19.4
Taxa	*Bregmaceros cantori*		13.5
	Saurida brasiliensis		8.0
	Hypsoblennius invemar	RA	6.0
	Synodus foetens		5.7
	Auxis spp.		4.2
	Decapterus punctatus		4.0
	Euthynnus alletteratus		3.7
	Ophichthus spp.		3.0
	Scartella/Hypleurochilus	RA	2.3
Reef Taxa	*Pomacentrus* spp.	RD	1.9
	Lutjanus spp.	RA	1.4
	Parablennius marmoreus	RA	1.2
	Hypsoblennius hentz/ionthas	RA	1.0
	Lutjanus campechanus	RA	0.8

GC 18 (230 m) - outer shelf

			%
Dominant	*Auxis* spp.		10.2
Taxa	Gobiidae		10.1
	Caranx hippos/latus		9.7
	Caranx crysos		6.6
	Symphurus spp.		6.4
	Ariomma spp.		6.0
	Cynoscion arenarius		5.6
	Euthynnus alletteratus		3.6
	Pristipomoides aquilonaris	RA	2.9
	Epinephelinae	RA	2.6
Reef Taxa	Anthinae	RA	2.3
	Holocentrus spp.	RA	1.8
	Pomacentrus spp.	RD	1.8
	Scaridae	RD	1.0

MP 259 (120 m) - outer shelf

			%
Dominant	*Auxis* spp.		19.1
Taxa	Gobiidae		13.7
	Caranx crysos		13.3
	Euthynnus alletteratus		8.6
	Myctophidae		6.6
	Bregmaceros cantori		3.8
	Synodus foetens		3.8
	Symphurus spp.		3.4
	Decapterus punctatus		2.5
	Microdesmus lanceolatus		2.1
Reef Taxa	*Hypsoblennius invemar*	RA	1.3
	Holocentrus spp.	RA	0.7
	Pomacentrus spp.	RD	0.5

Table 6. Mean densities and CPUEs (with standard errors) for taxa more abundant at platforms either east or west of the Mississippi River Delta in both plankton nets and light traps. Underlined means are significantly greater.

Mean plankton net densities (#/100 m^3)

Taxa	East of Delta	West of Delta	Wilcoxon 2-sample test
Decapterus punctatus	0.42 ± 0.24	0.02 ± 0.01	Z = 2.81, p=0.005
Eucinostomus spp.	1.15 ± 0.48	0	Z = 6.11, p=0.0001
Lutjanus spp.	1.45 ± 0.59	0.61 ± 0.20	Z = 2.83, p=0.005
Microdesmus lanceolatus	2.74 ± 0.49	1.19 ± 0.33	Z = 4.74, p=0.0001
Ophichthidae	2.06 ± 0.54	0.14 ± 0.07	Z = 5.67, p=0.0001
Thunnus spp.	0.50 ± 0.33	0.04 ± 0.03	Z = 1.16, p=0.25
Caranx hippos/latus	0.01 ± 0.01	1.77 ± 0.83	Z = -2.71, p=0.007
Cynoscion arenarius	4.54 ± 1.38	11.03 ± 2.37	Z = -0.65, p=0.51
Euthynnus alletteratus	2.27 ± 0.74	3.28 ± 0.70	Z = -0.33, p=0.74
Peprilus burti	0	0.56 ± 0.40	Z = -1.33, p=0.18
Scomberomorus cavalla	0.46 ± 0.13	1.84 ± 1.02	Z = -0.04, p=0.95
Symphurus spp.	2.37 ± 0.44	7.51 ± 1.47	Z = -0.77, p=0.44

Mean light trap CPUE (#/10 min.)

Taxa	East of Delta	West of Delta	Wilcoxon 2-sample test
Decapterus punctatus	0.58 ± 0.13	0.03 ± 0.01	Z = 8.26, p=0.0001
Eucinostomus spp.	0.38 ± 0.14	0.04 ± 0.01	Z = 6.09, p=0.0001
Lutjanus spp.	0.22 ± 0.11	0.01 ± 0.005	Z = 4.30, p=0.0001
Microdesmus lanceolatus	0.02 ± 0.01	0.006 ± 0.004	Z = 1.59, p=0.11
Ophichthidae	0.16 ± 0.03	0.03 ± 0.01	Z = 5.70, p=0.0001
Thunnus spp.	0.06 ± 0.02	0.02 ± 0.01	Z = 2.48, p=0.01
Caranx hippos/latus	0.01 ± 0.008	0.19 ± 0.04	Z = -4.02, p=0.0001
Cynoscion arenarius	0.01 ± 0.01	0.12 ± 0.03	Z = -3.14, p=0.002
Euthynnus alletteratus	0.55 ± 0.15	1.44 ± 0.23	Z = -2.71, p=0.007
Peprilus burti	0	0.05 ± 0.01	Z = -2.18, p=0.03
Scomberomorus cavalla	0.09 ± 0.03	0.15 ± 0.04	Z = -2.42, p=0.02
Symphurus spp.	0.02 ± 0.01	0.09 ± 0.02	Z = -2.67, p=0.008

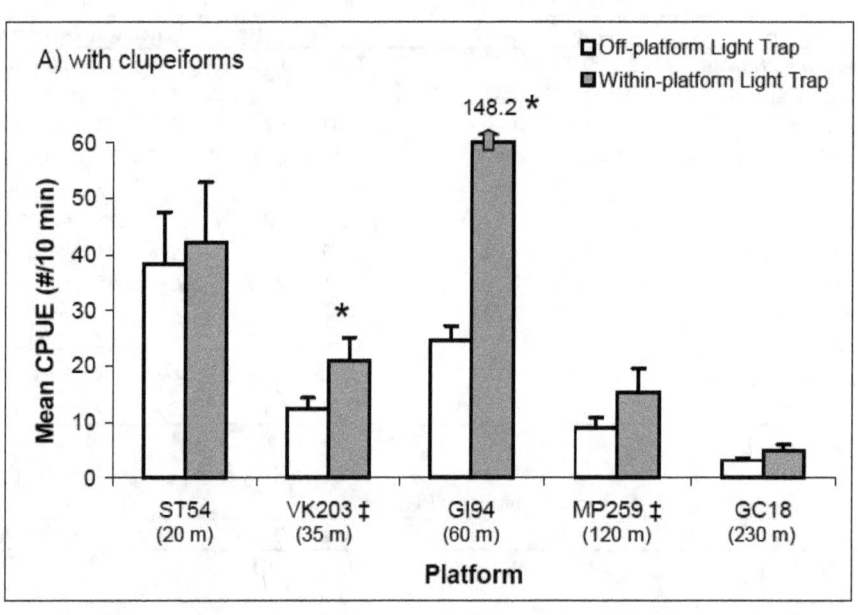

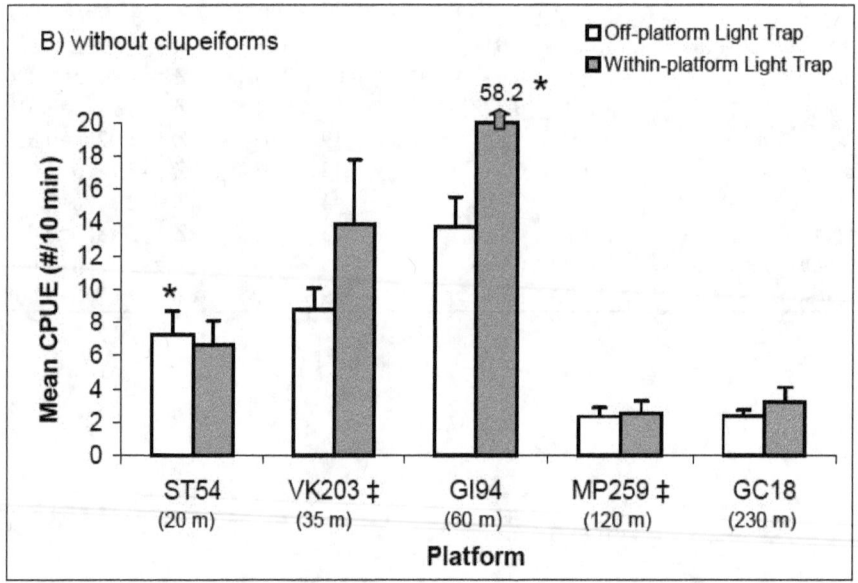

Figure 7. Mean CPUEs (with standard errors) from within- and off-platform light traps at each platform for data a) with clupeiforms and b) without clupeiforms. Arrows above the bars point to the mean for that gear. Asterisk denotes significant differences between light traps at a platform using the Wilcoxon 2-sample test. Numbers in parentheses indicate the depth, in meters, of each platform. ‡ denotes platforms East of the Delta.

Within- vs. Off-Platform Patterns in Light Trap Catches

Light traps fished within the platform structure generally had higher mean CPUEs than light traps fished down-current from the platform (Figure 7). With clupeiforms included, VK 203 ($Z = -1.97$, $p<0.05$) and GI 94 ($Z = 8.58$, $p<0.0001$) had significantly higher total catch rates within-platform. When clupeiforms were removed from these analyses, mean total CPUEs remained higher for within-platform light traps, with GI 94's significantly higher ($Z = 5.74$, $p<0.0001$). The exception was ST 54, where off-platform catch rates were significantly higher ($Z = 2.31$, $p<0.02$).

Comparisons of taxonomic richness and diversity between within- and off-platform light trap collections showed no clear patterns among platforms (Table 7). Within-platform light traps collected more families and taxa (identified to at least the genus level) than off-platform light traps at GC 18 and GI 94. However, slightly higher numbers of families and taxa were identified from off-platform collections at ST 54, VK 203 and MP 259 (number of taxa at MP 259 were equal). Mean Shannon-Wiener diversity indices were greater for within-platform light trap collections at GC 18 and GI 94, and significantly greater at VK 203 ($Z = 4.05$, $p<0.0001$). Off-platform light trap collections had greater diversity indices at ST 54 and MP 259.

Higher measures of similarity between the within- and off-platform fish assemblages coincided with relatively greater abundances of clupeiforms off-platform at ST 54 and MP 259. The fish assemblages collected by within- and off-platform light traps were most similar at ST 54 and MP 259 (Bray-Curtis similarity = 0.76 and 0.72, respectively) than at the other platforms (GC 18 = 0.49, GI 94 = 0.47, VK 203 = 0.47). Furthermore, only at ST 54 and MP 259 were mean off-platform CPUEs of clupeiforms not significantly lower than within-platform CPUEs (Table 8).

Fishes from the families Clupeidae (*Harengula jaguana* and *Opisthonema oglinum*), Engraulidae (*Anchoa mitchilli*, *A. nasuta/hepsetus* and *Engraulis eurystole*), Synodontidae (*Saurida brasiliensis* and *Synodus foetens*), and Blenniidae (*Hypsoblennius hentz/ionthas* and *Scartella/Hypleurochilus*) were found, with a few exceptions, to have higher mean CPUEs in within-platform light trap samples at each platform (Table 9). Conversely, Scombridae (*Euthynnus alletteratus*, *Scomberomorus cavalla* and *S. maculatus*) were more abundant off-platform at each platform, except at VK 203 where CPUEs for these species were higher within-platform. *Pomacentrus* spp. and *Hypsoblennius invemar* also seemed to have higher mean CPUEs off-platform, with the exception of GC 18 and GI 94, respectively. Mean CPUEs for *Caranx hippos/latus* were significantly higher in off-platform light traps at ST 54 and GC 18. Of the most abundant reef fish families, only Lutjanidae and Serranidae at GI 94 showed significant differences between mean light trap CPUEs, with both taxa being more abundant within-platform. Otherwise, reef fish CPUEs were low (<0.13 fish/10 min.) at each platform, except VK 203 where lutjanid CPUEs for within- and off-platform light traps were 0.35 and 0.55 fish/10 min., respectively.

Several species of engraulids showed significantly different size distributions between within- and off-platform light trap collections at platforms (Figure 8). Most *Anchoa mitchilli* collected within-platform at GI 94 were between 13 and 16 mm, while those collected off-platform were mainly 16 to 19 mm in length. Much larger *Engraulis eurystole* were collected in

Table 7. Taxonomic richness and mean Shannon-Weiner Diversity (with standard errors) for the larval and juvenile fish assemblages collected by within- (SL) and off-platform (OL) light traps at each platform. Numbers in parentheses indicate the depth, in meters, of each platform. ‡ denotes platforms east of the Delta.

	Light Trap	Families	Taxa	Diversity
GC18 (230 m)	SL	32	47	0.803 ± 0.090
	OL	28	37	0.699 ± 0.071
MP259 (120 m) ‡	SL	18	31	0.748 ± 0.067
	OL	20	31	0.923 ± 0.085
GI94 (60 m)	SL	34	71	1.162 ± 0.041
	OL	26	54	1.044 ± 0.051
VK203 (35 m) ‡	SL	26	53	1.454 ± 0.073
	OL	27	56	1.069 ± 0.058
ST54 (20 m)	SL	26	40	0.801 ± 0.064
	OL	27	51	0.875 ± 0.075

Table 8. Mean CPUEs (with standard errors) of clupeiforms from within- and off-platform light traps at each platform. Underlined means are significantly greater. Numbers in parentheses indicate the depth, in meter, of each platform. ‡ denotes platforms east of the Delta.

	Within-platform Light Trap	Off-platform Light Trap	Wilcoxon 2-sample test
GC18 (230 m)	1.73 ± 0.39	0.77 ± 0.22	Z = -2.33, p<0.02
MP259 (120 m) ‡	12.80 ± 4.17	6.55 ± 1.52	Z = -0.71, p<0.48
GI94 (60 m)	90.06 ± 25.83	10.85 ± 2.14	Z = 3.57, p<0.0004
VK203 (35 m) ‡	7.07 ± 1.22	3.57 ± 0.91	Z = -2.77, p<0.006
ST54 (20 m)	35.55 ± 10.56	31.04 ± 9.35	Z = 0.58, p<0.56

Table 9. Mean CPUEs of the dominant taxa, and reef fish families, from within- and off-platform light traps at each platform. Underlined mean CPUEs are significantly greater for taxa at a platform (Wilcoxon 2-sample test, p<0.05). Numbers in parentheses indicate the depth, in meters, of each platform. ‡ denotes platforms east of the Delta. RA = reef associated taxa; RD = reef dependent taxa.

Dominant Taxa		ST54 (20 m)		VK203 (35 m) ‡		GI94 (60 m)		MP259 (120 m) ‡		GC18 (230 m)	
		Within Platform	Off Platform	Within Platform	Off Platform	Within Platform	Off Platform	Within Platform	Off Platform	Within Platform	Off Platform
Harengula jaguana		0.56	0.55	2.05	1.97	0.69	0.68	0.53	0.50	0.15	0
Opisthonema oglinum		23.26	25.53	1.27	0.08	6.04	4.11	5.34	2.39	0.42	0.28
Anchoa mitchilli		0.38	0.31	0.02	0.02	1.89	0.47	0.16	0.11	0.15	0
Anchoa nasuta/hepsetus		9.96	3.69	0.93	0.07	41.91	3.26	0.47	0.70	0.22	0.16
Engraulis eurystole		0.26	0.03	1.80	0.17	38.79	1.25	5.98	2.38	0.25	0.02
Saurida brasiliensis		0.06	0.08	2.57	0.36	3.35	0.50	0.16	0	0.20	0
Synodus foetens		3.16	0.27	2.57	0.03	22.11	0.20	0.90	0.05	0	0
Caranx crysos		0.07	0.24	0.43	0.17	0.08	0.08	0.16	0.18	0.24	0.30
Caranx hippos/latus		0.04	0.61	0.02	0	0.11	0.09	0.03	0	0.08	0.22
Decapterus punctatus		0.02	0.02	1.28	0.69	0.06	0.01	0.09	0.11	0.01	0
Pomacentrus spp.	RD	0	0.02	0.35	0.51	0.12	0.30	0.04	0.07	0.14	0.03
Hypsoblennius hentz/ionthas	RA	0.21	0.48	0.30	0.12	1.76	0.04	0	0	0	0
Hypsoblennius invemar	RA	0.11	0.48	0.23	2.46	6.33	3.58	0.03	0.38	0	0.01
Scartella/Hypleurochilus	RA	0.49	0.16	0.38	0.25	1.14	0.11	0	0	0	0
Auxis spp.		0.02	0.26	0.67	1.19	0.76	0.24	0.19	0.13	0.40	0.14
Euthynnus alletteratus		0.37	1.08	1.17	0.40	0.92	2.83	0.10	0.29	0.06	0.18
Scomberomorus cavalla		0.05	0.10	0.23	0.05	0.09	0.27	0.01	0.04	0.02	0.03
Scomberomorus maculatus		0.18	0.81	0.42	0.14	0.04	0.17	0.01	0.05	0	0.02
Reef families											
Holocentridae	RA	0	0	0	0	0	0.01	0.13	0.07	0.07	0.11
Lutjanidae	RA	0	0.02	0.35	0.55	0.11	0.02	0	0.02	0.04	0.01
Serranidae	RA	0.01	0	0.03	0.03	0.12	0	0.03	0.04	0.02	0.02

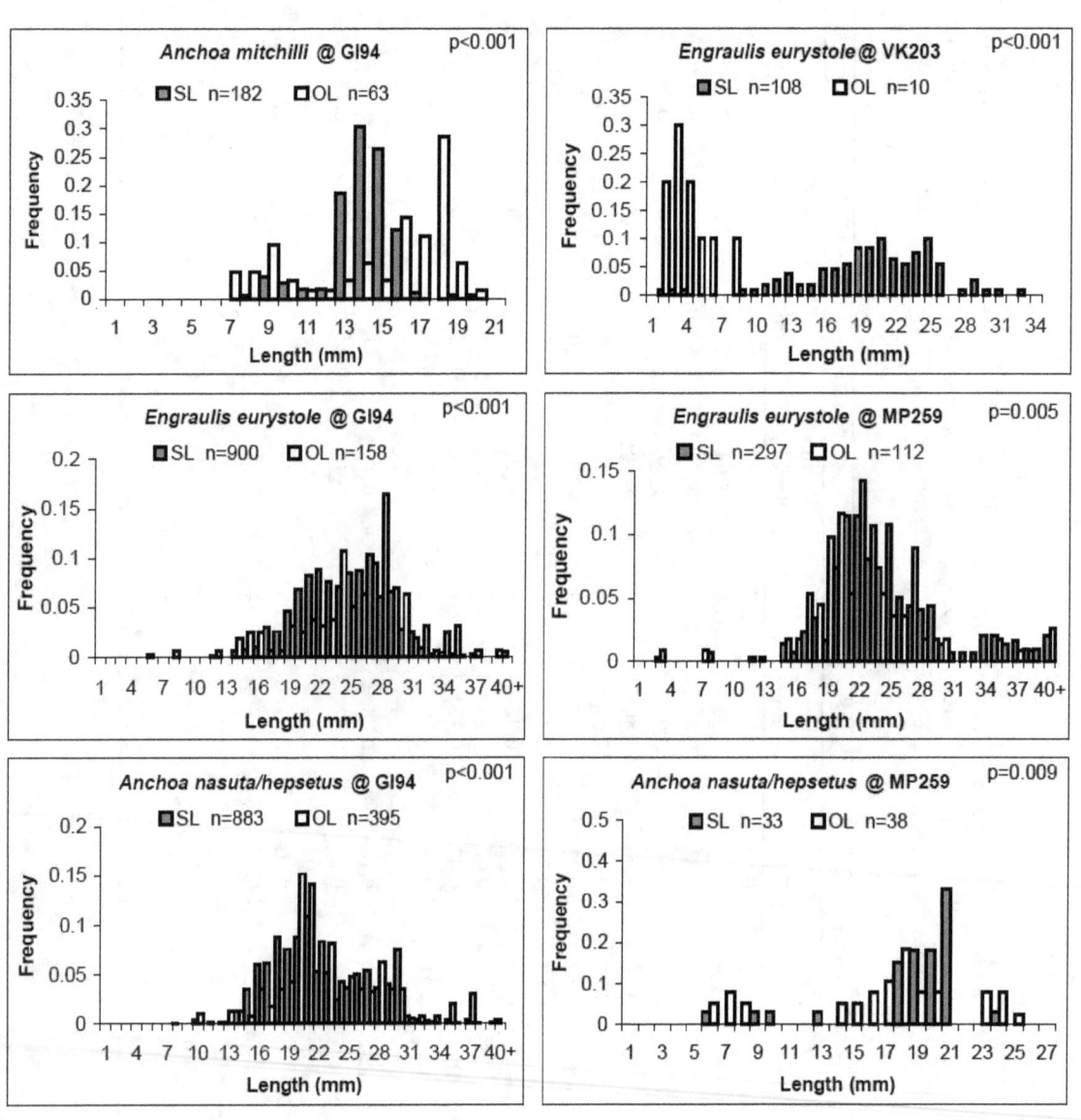

Figure 8. Significantly different size distributions of engraulids collected by off-platform (OL) and within-platform (SL) light traps. Number of samples (n) and the p-values from K-S Tests are included.

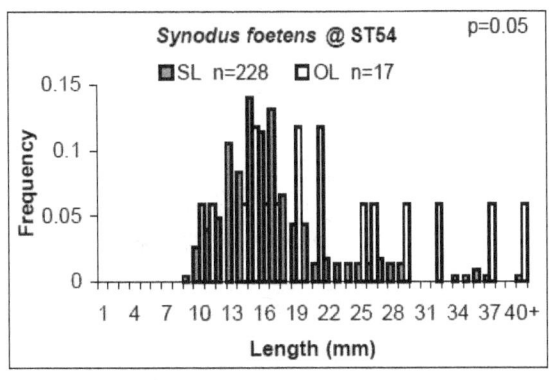
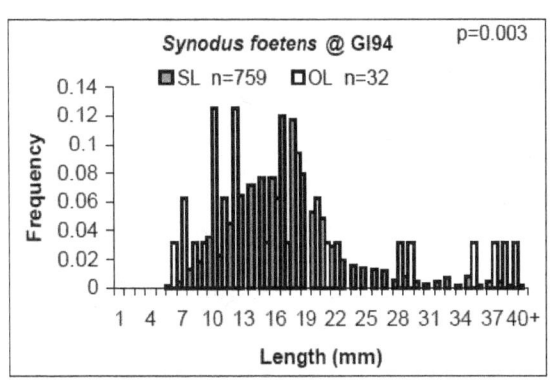
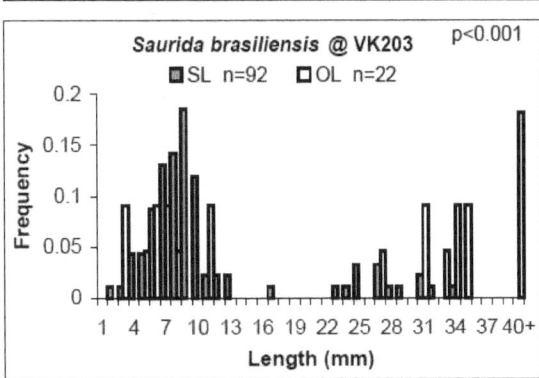
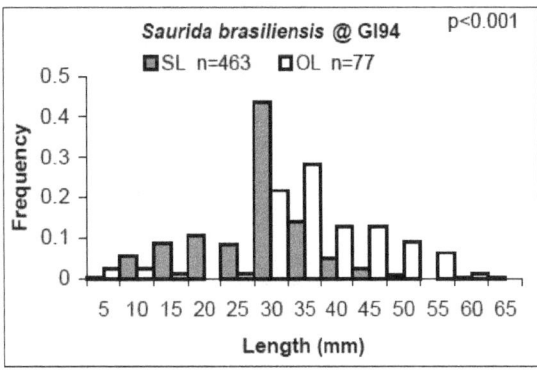

Figure 9. Significantly different size distributions of synodontids collected by off-platform (OL) and within-platform (SL) light traps. Number of samples (n) and the p-values from K-S Tests are included.

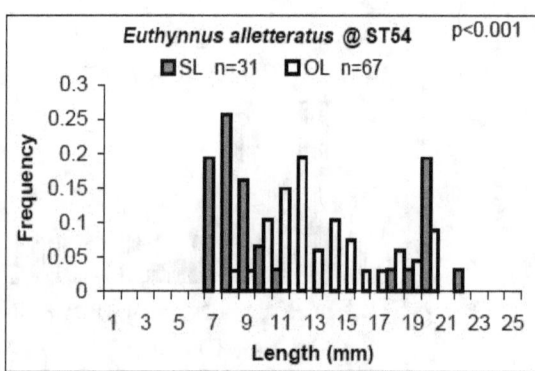

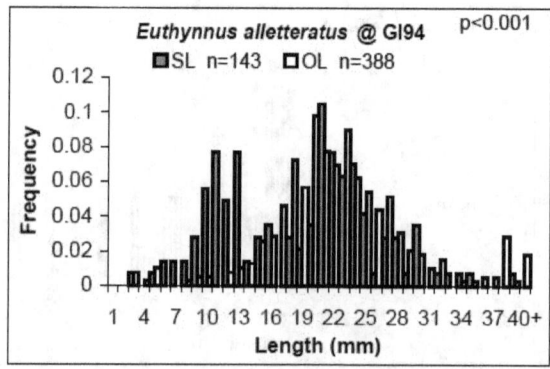

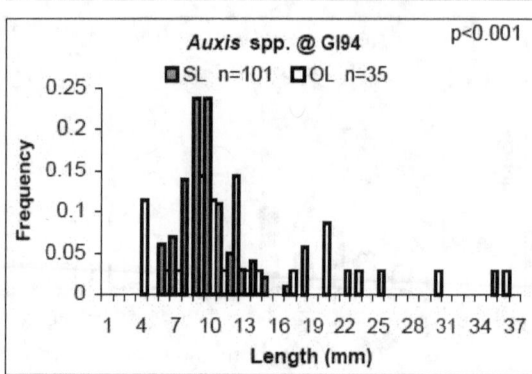

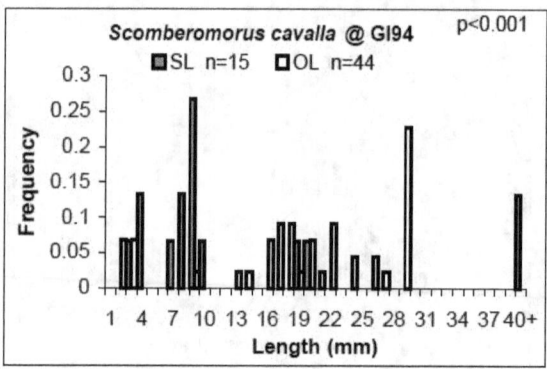

Figure 10. Significantly different size distributions of scombrids collected by off-platform (OL) and within-platform (SL) light traps. Number of samples (n) and the p-values from K-S Tests are included.

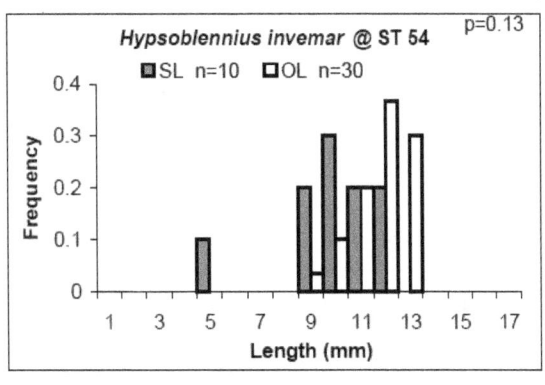

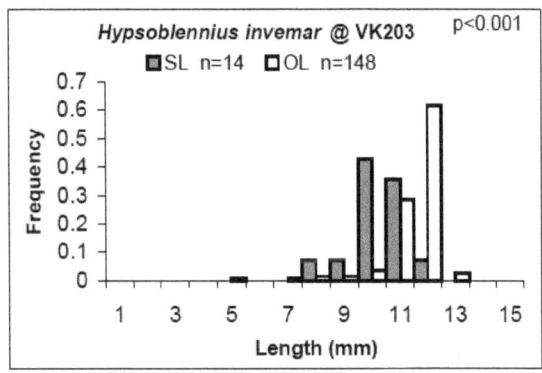

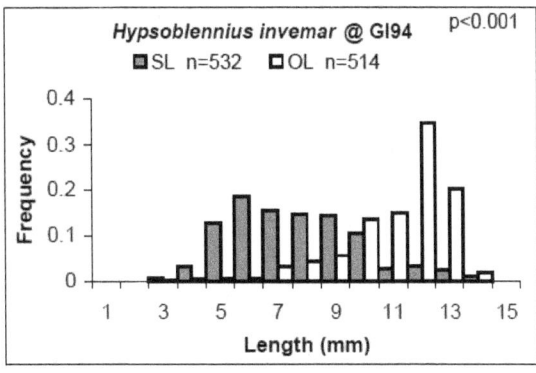

Figure 11. Significantly different size distributions of *Hypsoblennius invemar* collected by off-platform (OL) and within-platform (SL) light traps. Also presented are size distributions of *H. invemar* from the inner shelf platform, ST 54. Number of samples (n) and the p-values from K-S Tests are included.

39

within-platform light traps at VK 203, while off-platform light traps only collected fish ≤ 8 mm. Although the size distributions of *E. eurystole* at GI 94 and MP 259 overlapped considerably, the median length was slightly larger off-platform than within-platform (27 vs. 24 mm at GI 94, 23 vs. 22 at MP 259). Median lengths of *Anchoa nasuta/hepsetus* were larger off-platform at GI 94 (22 vs. 21 mm), while at MP 259 the median length was larger within-platform (20 vs. 18 mm).

Significantly different size distributions were also found for synodontids in comparisons of within- and off-platform light trap collections (Figure 9). *Synodus foetens* collected off-platform at ST 54 and GI 94 had a greater frequency of larger individuals (>28 mm) than within-platform collections; however, caution should be exercised considering the disproportionately larger numbers taken within-platform at both locations. Larger individuals of *Saurida brasiliensis* were also more frequent in off-platform collections at VK 203 and GI 94.

Size distributions of scombrids in off-platform light trap collections generally encompassed larger size classes than within-platform light traps (Figure 10). *Euthynnus alletteratus* collected in within-platform light traps at ST 54 and GI 94 were generally taken in two modes, including a mode around 7 to 13 mm that was absent in off-platform light traps. Size distributions of *Auxis* spp. and *Scomberomorus cavalla* collected off-platform at GI 94 had greater frequencies of larger individuals (>15 mm) than within-platform collections.

Larger *Hypsoblennius invemar* were found in off-platform light traps, as compared with within-platform light traps (Figure 11). The size distributions of *H. invemar* in off-platform collections had a median length of 12 mm at each platform, while in within-platform collections the median was 10 mm, except at GI 94 where the median length was 7 mm for within-platform collections.

Few reef taxa were collected in sufficient numbers to compare size distributions between within- and off-platform light traps. No statistically significant size differences were found for the blenniids *Hypsoblennius hentz/ionthas* and *Scartella/Hypleurochilus* at ST 54, VK 203 or GI 94, as was also the situation for *Pomacentrus* spp. at VK 203 and GI 94. Although they were not collected in sufficient numbers to analyze statistically, the median lengths of *Holocentrus* spp. were larger within-platform at MP 259 (13 vs. 10 mm) and GC 18 (31 vs. 22.5 mm). All other reef taxa were collected at similar sizes between within- and off-platform light traps.

Comparisons of Within-, and 20 m and 50 m Off-Platform Light Trap Catches

On three occasions at VK 203, samples were collected using light traps deployed at three distances relative to the platform: within the platform; 20 m down-current from the platform; and 50 m down-current from the platform. Total mean CPUEs were highest for the 50 m off-platform (19.00 ± 6.66) and 20 m off-platform light traps (17.10 ± 5.36), as compared with the within-platform light trap (13.20 ± 2.25). The higher catch rates off-platform were mostly the result of high CPUEs during the July 29 sampling effort, when large numbers of the blenniid *Hypsoblennius invemar* were collected (Figure 12). When this species was removed from the data, total mean CPUEs were significantly higher for the within-platform light trap (12.40 ± 2.23), as compared with the 20 m off-platform (6.40 ± 0.85) and 50 m off-platform light traps (6.20 ± 1.36; Kruskal-Wallis $\chi^2 = 7.29$, p<0.03).

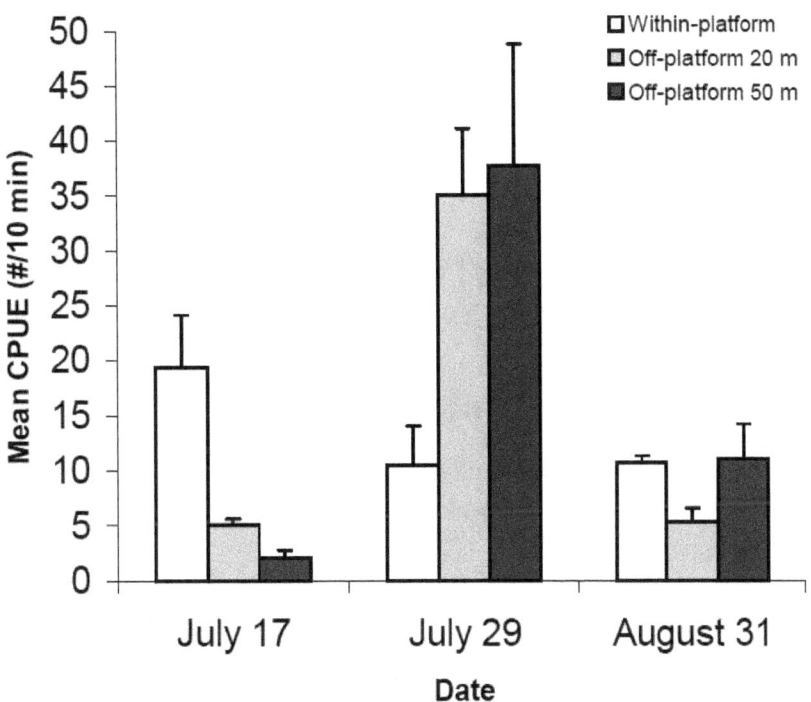

Figure 12. Mean total CPUEs (with standard errors) by sampling date from light traps deployed at three distances relative to the mid-shelf platform VK 203: within the platform, 20 m down-current from the platform, and 50 m down-current from the platform.

Table 10. Mean CPUE (fish/10 min) for fish collected using light traps at three distances relative to the mid-shelf platform VK 203, with standard error (SE), rank, and percent of total catch (%N). RA= reef associated taxa, RD= reef dependent taxa.

TAXA	Within-Platform Light Trap CPUE (SE) Rank (%N)	Off-Platform Light Trap (20 m) CPUE (SE) Rank (%N)	Off-Platform Light Trap (50 m) CPUE (SE) Rank (%N)
Anguilliformes			
Ophichthidae			
Ophichthus gomesi (shrimp eel)	0.20 (0.13) 14 (1.53)	0 (0)	0 (0)
Clupeiformes			
Clupeidae			
Harengula jaguana (scaled sardine)	1.10 (0.41) 5 (8.40)	0.10 (0.10) 14(0.57)	0.30 (0.15) 4.5 (1.57)
Opisthonema oglinum (Atlantic thread herring)	2.50 (0.97) 1(19.08)	1.00 (0.54) 3 (5.68)	0 (0)
Sardinella aurita (Spanish sardine)	0.10 (0.10) 19 (0.76)	0 (0)	0 (0)
Engraulidae			
Unidentified	0.40 (0.22) 10 (3.05)	2.67 (0.51) 2 (16.48)	3.77 (1.03) 2 (20.42)
Anchoa nasuta/hepsetus (longnose/striped anchovy)	1.70 (0.63) 2.5 (12.98)	0.30 (0.16) 5 (2.27)	0 (0)
Anchoa mitchilli (bay anchovy)	0.40 (0.31) 10 (3.05)	0.10 (0.10) 14 (0.57)	0 (0)
Anchoviella perfasciata (flat anchovy)	1.40 (0.62) 4 (10.69)	0 (0)	0 (0)
Engraulis eurystole (silver anchovy)	0.70 (0.33) 6.5 (5.34)	0 (0)	0 (0)
Aulopiformes			
Synodontidae			
Saurida brasiliensis (largescale lizardfish)	1.70 (0.88) 2.5 (12.98)	0.07 (0.07) 19.5 (0.57)	0.07 (0.07) 13.5 (0.52)
Synodus foetens (inshore lizardfish)	0.50 (0.17) 8 (3.82)	0 (0)	0 (0)
Gadiformes			
Bregmacerotidae			
Bregmaceros cantori (codlet)	0 (0)	0 (0)	0.07 (0.07) 13.5 (0.52)
Scorpaeniformes			
Triglidae			
Unidentified (searobins)	0.10 (0.10) 19 (0.76)	0 (0)	0 (0)

Table 10. (continued)

TAXA	Within-Platform Light Trap	Off-Platform Light Trap (20 m)	Off-Platform Light Trap (50 m)
	CPUE (SE) Rank (%N)	CPUE (SE) Rank (%N)	CPUE (SE) Rank (%N)
Perciformes			
Carangidae			
Caranx crysos (blue runner)	0 (0)	0 (0)	0.10 (0.10) 9.5 (0.52)
Caranx latus (horse-eye jack)	0 (0)	0 (0)	0.10 (0.10) 9.5 (0.52)
Chloroscombrus chrysurus (Atlantic bumper)	0.10 (0.10) 19 (0.76)	0.20 (0.20) 6.5 (1.14)	0.90 (0.35) 3 (4.71)
Decapterus punctatus (round scad)	0.40 (0.22) 10 (3.05)	0.10 (0.10) 14 (0.57)	0 (0)
Lutjanidae (RA)			
Lutjanus spp.	0 (0)	0.70 (0.33) 4 (3.98)	0 (0)
Lutjanus synagris (lane snapper)	0 (0)	0.10 (0.10) 14 (0.57)	0 (0)
Rhomboplites aurorubens (vermilion snapper)	0.10 (0.10) 19 (0.76)	0 (0)	0.10 (0.10) 9.5 (0.52)
Gerreidae			
Unidentified (mojarras)	0 (0)	0.10 (0.10) 14 (0.57)	0 (0)
Sciaenidae			
Cynoscion arenarius (sand seatrout)	0.10 (0.10) 19 (0.76)	0 (0)	0.10 (0.10) 9.5 (0.52)
Pomacentridae (RD)			
Pomacentrus spp. (damselfishes)	0.10 (0.10) 19 (0.76)	0 (0)	0.20 (0.13) 6 (1.05)
Sphyraenidae			
Sphyraena guachancho (guaguanche)	0 (0)	0.10 (0.10) 14 (0.57)	0 (0)
Blenniidae (RA)			
Unidentified	0 (0)	0.10 (0.10) 14 (0.57)	0 (0)
Hypsoblennius hentz/ionthas (feather/freckled blenny)	0.10 (0.10) 19 (0.76)	0 (0)	0 (0)
Hypsoblennius invemar (tesselated blenny)	0.70 (0.30) 6.5 (5.34)	10.70 (4.72) 1 (60.80)	12.70 (6.28) 1 (66.49)
Gobiidae			
Unidentified (gobies)	0.20 (0.13) 14 (1.53)	0.13 (0.09) 9 (1.14)	0.10 (0.10) 9.5 (0.52)
Scombridae			
Euthynnus alletteratus (little tunny)	0.20 (0.20) 14 (1.53)	0.20 (0.13) 6.5 (1.14)	0 (0)
Scomberomorus maculatus (Spanish mackerel)	0.30 (0.21) 12 (2.29)	0.17 (0.11) 8 (1.14)	0.10 (0.10) 9.5 (0.52)

Table 10. (continued)

TAXA	Within-Platform Light Trap CPUE (SE) Rank (%N)	Off-Platform Light Trap (20 m) CPUE (SE) Rank (%N)	Off-Platform Light Trap (50 m) CPUE (SE) Rank (%N)
Pleuronectiformes			
Cynoglossidae			
Symphurus civitatus (offshore tonguefish)	0 (0)	0.10 (0.10) 14 (0.57)	0 (0)
Bothidae			
Syacium spp. (dusky/shoal flounder)	0 (0)	0.10 (0.10) 14 (0.57)	0.30 (0.21) 4.5 (1.57)
Tetraodontiformes			
Tetraodontidae			
Unidentified (puffers)	0 (0)	0.07 (0.07) 19.5 (0.57)	0 (0)

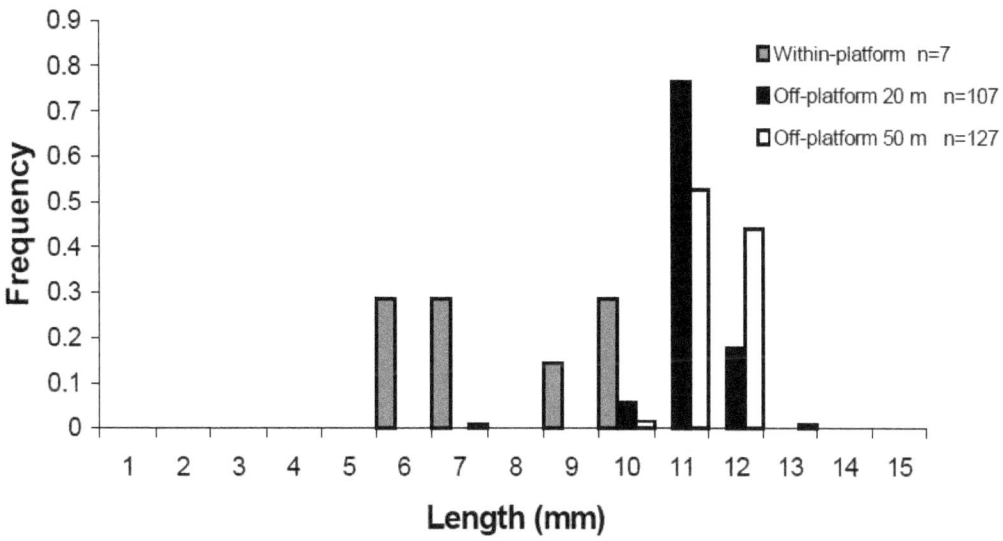

Figure 13. Size distributions of *Hypsoblennius invemar* collected at VK 203 using light traps deployed at three distances relative to the platform: within the platform, 20 m down-current from the platform, and 50 m down-current from the platform.

A total of 498 fishes, from 18 families, was collected from 30 light trap samples (10 for each light trap distance; Table 10). Within-platform light traps collected a total of 19 taxa (identified to at least the genus level), while the 20 m off-platform collected 15 taxa and the 50 m off-platform collected 12 taxa. Mean Shannon-Wiener diversity indices were significantly higher for the within-platform light trap (1.49 ± 0.14) than the 20 m off-platform (0.67 ± 0.08) or the 50 m off-platform (0.56 ± 0.20; $\chi^2 = 12.75$, p<0.002). The within-platform catch was predominantly composed of clupeiforms (63.4% of the total catch) and synodontids (16.8%), while *Hypsoblennius invemar*, *Decapterus punctatus* and *Scomberomorus cavalla* were minor components of the catch. The 20 m and 50 m off-platform catches were dominated by *H. invemar* (60.8% and 66.5%, respectively), although preflexion engraulids, *Lutjanus* spp. and *Chloroscombrus chrysurus* were also abundant.

Because of the low number of samples, few taxa were found in sufficient numbers to compare size distributions across the three light trap distances. Kolmogorov-Smirnov tests of the sizes of *Hypsoblennius invemar* found each size distribution significantly different from each other (P<0.0005; Figure 13). Sizes of *H. invemar* within-platform were between 6 and 10 mm, while in both 20 m and 50 m off-platform light traps the sizes were predominantly 11 to 12 mm. *Anchoa nasuta/hepsetus* were larger in within-platform (median = 16 mm) than the 20 m off-platform light trap collections (6 mm). Although sample size was low, the sizes of *Euthynnus alletteratus* collected in the 20 m off-platform light trap were >40 mm in length, while within-platform individuals collected were 9 and 11 mm. The sizes of other taxa were generally similar across light trap distances.

Comparisons of SEAMAP vs. Platform Collections

Reef-dependent taxa were relatively rare, as compared with reef-associated taxa, in both platform plankton nets and SEAMAP bongo nets west of the Delta (Table 11). On the outer shelf, reef-dependent families Pomacentridae, Labridae, Acanthuridae, and Scaridae were present only in SEAMAP collections, while chaetodontids were only found in platform collections. In contrast, reef-dependent taxa were only found in platform collections at mid-shelf (i.e., Chaetodontidae, Pomacentridae and Labridae) and inner shelf (i.e., Scaridae), albeit in low densities. Reef-associated taxa were taken in larger densities in platform collections at all shelf locations with the exception of serranids, which had higher densities in SEAMAP collections. East of the Delta, labrids and scarids were the predominant reef-dependent taxa collected, and were more common in SEAMAP bongo net collections (Table 12). Of the reef-associated taxa, lutjanids and serranids were found in higher densities in SEAMAP collections, while blenniids had higher densities in platform collections.

Significantly different size distributions were found for serranids between SEAMAP bongo net and platform plankton net collections, with slightly smaller median lengths in SEAMAP collections (2 mm vs. 3; Figure 14). Lutjanids also displayed significantly different size distributions, having once again slightly smaller median lengths in SEAMAP collections (2 mm vs. 4; Figure 15). Statistical comparisons between ST 54, GI 94 and their respective SEAMAP samples were not possible for serranids and lutjanids due to limited numbers collected. No significant differences were found between the size distributions of labrids collected at MP 259 and nearby SEAMAP stations, as both distributions ranged from 1 to 6 mm.

Table 11. Mean abundance (fish/m²), with standard deviation (SD), for reef fish collected at selected nearby SEAMAP ichthyoplankton sampling stations (oblique, 60-cm bongo tows) and at three oil and gas platforms (passively-fished, 60-cm plankton nets, surface and subsurface) across the continental shelf west of the Delta.

	Inner Shelf		Mid-shelf		Outer Shelf	
	SEAMAP[†] Mean (SD)	ST 54‡ Mean (SD)	SEAMAP[†] Mean (SD)	GI 94‡ Mean (SD)	SEAMAP[†] Mean (SD)	GC 18‡ Mean (SD)
Reef-dependent						
Chaetodontidae	0 (0)	0 (0)	0 (0)	<0.1 (0.5)	0 (0)	0.8 (0.7)
Pomacanthidae	0 (0)	0 (0)	0 (0)	0 (0)	0 (0)	0 (0)
Pomacentridae	0 (0)	0 (0)	0 (0)	1.1 (6.7)	1.3 (4.0)	0 (0)
Labridae	0 (0)	0 (0)	0 (0)	<0.1 (0.8)	4.4 (7.2)	0 (0)
Acanthuridae	0 (0)	0 (0)	0 (0)	0 (0)	0.3 (1.5)	0 (0)
Scaridae	0 (0)	0.5 (1.3)	0 (0)	0 (0)	1.6 (3.7)	0 (0)
Reef-associated						
Holocentridae	0 (0)	0 (0)	0 (0)	0.3 (1.7)	0.3 (1.2)	0.6 (1.5)
Serranidae	0.2 (0.7)	0 (0)	5.6 (5.0)	1.2 (3.4)	72.3 (83.2)	3.0 (3.9)
Lutjanidae	0 (0)	0 (0)	1.9 (5.4)	2.1 (6.7)	3.2 (5.1)	8.2 (12.6)
Blenniidae	0.7 (2.0)	1.2 (2.4)	3.2 (5.4)	17.6 (19.3)	0 (0)	4.1 (13.3)

†Means calculated for five outer shelf (n=21), two mid-shelf (n=8) and three inner shelf (n=12) SEAMAP sampling stations (1995-1997).
‡Means calculated for paired (subsurface and surface), passive plankton net samples collected at GC 18 (n=14), GI 94 (n=161) and ST 54 (n=7), during 1995-1997.

47

Table 12. Mean abundance (fish/100 m^3), with standard deviation (SD), for reef fish collected at selected nearby SEAMAP ichthyoplankton sampling stations (oblique, 60-cm bongo tows) and at two oil and gas platforms (passively-fished, 60-cm surface plankton nets) across the continental shelf east of the Delta.

	Mid-shelf		Outer Shelf	
	SEAMAP[†] Mean (SD)	VK 203[‡] Mean (SD)	SEAMAP[†] Mean (SD)	MP 259[‡] Mean (SD)
Reef-dependent				
Chaetodontidae	0 (0)	0 (0)	0 (0)	0 (0)
Pomacanthidae	0 (0)	0 (0)	0 (0)	0 (0)
Pomacentridae	0 (0)	0 (0)	<0.1 (0.1)	0 (0)
Labridae	3.9 (8.8)	0 (0)	2.2 (2.9)	0.4 (1.3)
Acanthuridae	0 (0)	0 (0)	0 (0)	0 (0)
Scaridae	0 (0)	0 (0)	0.5 (0.7)	0.1 (0.6)
Reef-associated				
Holocentridae	0 (0)	0 (0)	0 (0)	0 (0)
Serranidae	18.3 (28.3)	1.1 (2.5)	1.0 (0.9)	0.6 (1.6)
Lutjanidae	3.5 (4.8)	1.8 (4.7)	2.6 (3.5)	0.4 (1.4)
Blenniidae	<0.1 (0.2)	4.8 (7.9)	0.1 (0.3)	2.1 (4.5)

[†]Means calculated for three outer shelf (n=5) and three mid-shelf (n=9) SEAMAP sampling stations (1995-1997).
[‡]Means calculated for passive surface plankton net samples collected at MP 259 (n=70) and VK 203 (n=60), during 1999-2000.

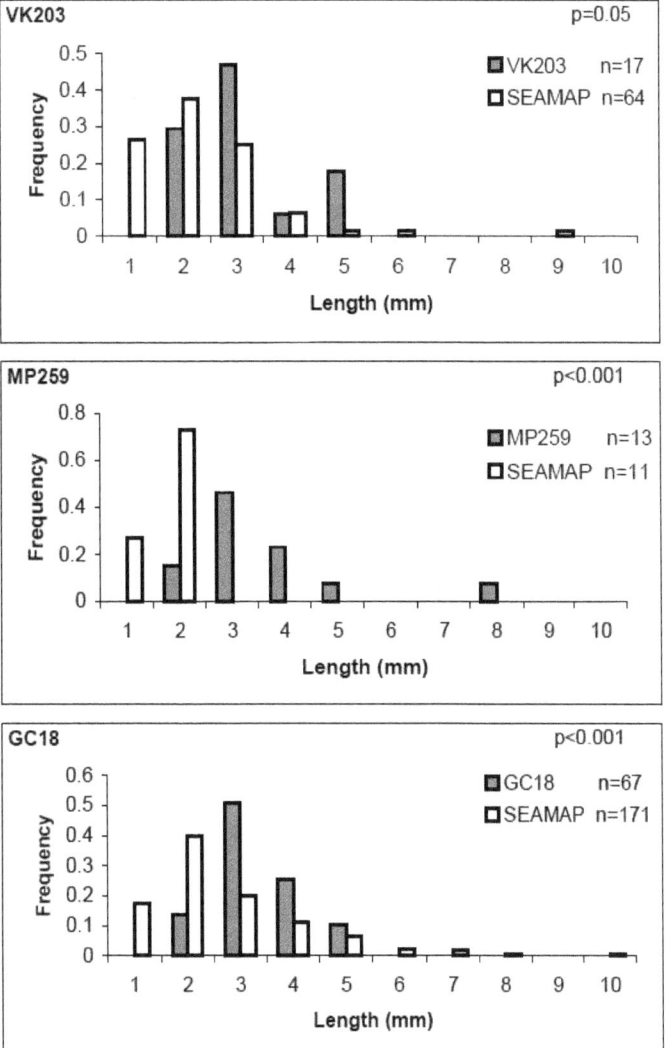

Figure 14. Significantly different size distributions of Serranidae
collected at platforms using passively-fished surface and
subsurface plankton nets, and at selected nearby SEAMAP
sampling stations using oblique bongo net tows. ‡ denotes
platforms east of the Delta where only surface collections
were taken. Number of samples (n) and the p-values from
K-S tests are included.

49

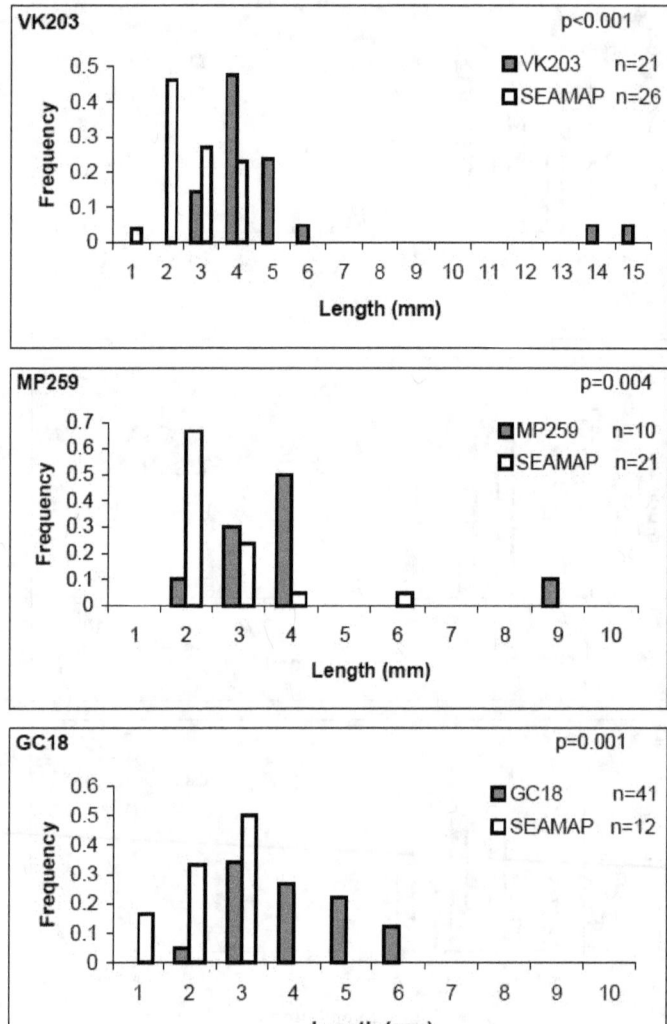

Figure 15. Significantly different size distributions of Lutjanidae collected at platforms using passively-fished surface and subsurface plankton nets, and at selected nearby SEAMAP sampling stations using oblique bongo net tows. ‡ denotes platforms east of the Delta where only surface collections were taken. Number of samples (n) and the p-values from K-S tests are included.

Table 13. Mean number (fish/sample), with standard deviation (SD), for reef fish collected at selected nearby SEAMAP ichthyoplankton sampling stations (neuston tows) and at three platforms (light-traps, within- and off-platform) across the continental shelf west of the Delta.

	Inner Shelf		Mid-shelf		Outer Shelf	
	SEAMAP† Mean (SD)	ST 54‡ Mean (SD)	SEAMAP† Mean (SD)	GI 94‡ Mean (SD)	SEAMAP† Mean (SD)	GC 18‡ Mean (SD)
Reef-dependent						
Chaetodontidae	0 (0)	0 (0)	0.1 (0.4)	0 (0)	0 (0)	0 (0)
Pomacanthidae	0 (0)	0 (0)	0 (0)	0 (0)	0 (0)	0 (0)
Pomacentridae	0 (0)	<0.1 (0.4)	0 (0)	0.5 (1.9)	0.2 (1.0)	0.1 (1.0)
Labridae	0 (0)	0 (0)	0 (0)	<0.1 (0.1)	<0.1 (0.2)	0 (0)
Acanthuridae	0 (0)	0 (0)	0 (0)	0 (0)	0 (0)	0 (0)
Scaridae	0 (0)	0 (0)	0 (0)	0 (0)	0 (0)	<0.1 (0.3)
Reef-associated						
Holocentridae	0 (0)	0 (0)	0 (0)	<0.1 (0.1)	0 (0)	0.1 (0.5)
Serranidae	0 (0)	<0.1 (0.1)	0 (0)	0.1 (0.4)	1.7 (5.6)	<0.1 (0.2)
Lutjanidae	0.3 (0.6)	<0.1 (0.1)	0.9 (2.1)	0.1 (0.3)	0.2 (0.7)	<0.1 (0.2)
Blenniidae	0.6 (1.0)	1.0 (3.5)	1.0 (1.4)	11.2 (31.1)	0.4 (1.6)	0.1 (1.4)

†Means calculated for five outer shelf (n=25), two mid-shelf (n=8) and three inner shelf (n=12) SEAMAP sampling stations (1995-1997).
‡Means calculated for light-trap (surface and off-platform) samples collected at GC 18 (n=154), GI 94 (n=319) and ST 54 (n=146), during 1995-1997.

Table 14. Mean number (fish/sample), with standard deviation (SD), for reef fish collected at selected nearby SEAMAP ichthyoplankton sampling stations (neuston tows) and at two platforms (light traps, within- and off-platform) across the continental shelf east of the Delta.

	Mid-shelf		Outer Shelf	
	SEAMAP† Mean (SD)	VK 203‡ Mean (SD)	SEAMAP† Mean (SD)	MP 259‡ Mean (SD)
Reef-dependent				
Chaetodontidae	0 (0)	0 (0)	0 (0)	0 (0)
Pomacanthidae	0 (0)	0 (0)	0 (0)	0 (0)
Pomacentridae	0.2 (0.4)	0.4 (1.0)	1.4 (3.2)	<0.1 (0.3)
Labridae	0.1 (0.3)	0 (0)	1.0 (2.2)	0 (0)
Acanthuridae	0 (0)	0 (0)	0 (0)	0 (0)
Scaridae	0 (0)	0 (0)	0 (0)	0 (0)
Reef-associated				
Holocentridae	0 (0)	0 (0)	0.2 (0.5)	0.1 (0.4)
Serranidae	0 (0)	<0.1 (0.2)	2.0 (3.9)	<0.1 (0.2)
Lutjanidae	0 (0)	0.5 (1.5)	1.0 (1.4)	<0.1 (0.1)
Blenniidae	11.2 (33.7)	2.2 (4.9)	0 (0)	0.2 (1.1)

†Means calculated for three outer shelf (n=5) and three mid-shelf (n=9) SEAMAP sampling stations (1995-1997).
‡Means calculated for light-trap (within- and off-platform) samples collected at MP 259 (n=126) and MP 259 (n=120), during 1999-2000.

Other reef taxa such as scarids, holocentrids and blenniids were collected at similar sizes between platform and SEAMAP samples.

Pomacentrids and labrids were the most common reef-dependent taxa collected by either SEAMAP neuston nets or platform light traps west of the Delta (Table 13). These taxa were more abundant in SEAMAP collections on the outer shelf and in platform collections on the mid and inner shelf, except for labrids which were absent on the inner shelf altogether. Of the reef-associated taxa only lutjanids were more abundant in SEAMAP collections than in platform collections. Blenniids and serranids were more abundant at platforms at the mid and inner shelf locations, but were more abundant at SEAMAP stations on the outer shelf. East of the Delta, pomacentrids and labrids were the only reef-dependent taxa collected (Table 14). Pomacentrids were more abundant in SEAMAP collections on the outer shelf, and in platform collections at mid-shelf. Labrids were only found in SEAMAP collections at either location. Reef-associated taxa were relatively rare on the outer shelf, and all but blenniids were more abundant in SEAMAP collections. In contrast, at mid-shelf, blenniids were the only taxa more abundant in SEAMAP neuston nets than in platform light traps.

No taxa were collected in sufficient numbers to statistically compare size distributions between neuston nets and light traps. In general, neuston nets and light traps collected similar size ranges, although light traps did collect more, larger individuals. For example, lengths of serranids collected in light traps at MP 259 ranged from 14 to 20 mm, while in corresponding SEAMAP neuston nets lengths ranged from 3 to 9 mm.

Seasonal Patterns of Plankton Net and Light Trap Catches

Mean total plankton net densities by trip at the outer shelf platform MP 259 ranged from 69-1706 fish/100 m^3 and peaked during late July (Figure 16). After clupeiforms were removed the July peak remained, while total densities were less than 80 fish/100 m^3 for all other sampling dates. Mean total light trap CPUEs by trip ranged from 1-68 fish/10 min. for both within- and off-platform collections and peaked during early July and late August (Figure 17). As with the plankton nets, when clupeiforms were removed light trap CPUEs remained highest during July, while CPUEs were low (<3 fish/10 min) on all other dates.

Mean total plankton net densities by trip at the mid-shelf platform VK 203 ranged from 67-1207 fish/100 m^3 and peaked at the end of August (Figure 18). When clupeiforms were removed, the highest mean densities occurred during early October. Mean total light trap CPUEs ranged from 3-62 fish/10 min. for both within- and off-platform collections and peaked during June (Figure 19). Removing clupeiforms from the catches did little to change these patterns.

Lunar Periodicity

Mean total plankton net densities were higher, though not significantly, during full moons than new moons at the outer shelf platform MP 259 (Figure 20). When clupeiforms were removed, the mean density was only slightly higher during full moons. Mean total light trap CPUEs were also higher during full moons, but when clupeiforms were removed CPUEs were higher during new moons. At the mid-shelf platform VK 203, mean total plankton net densities

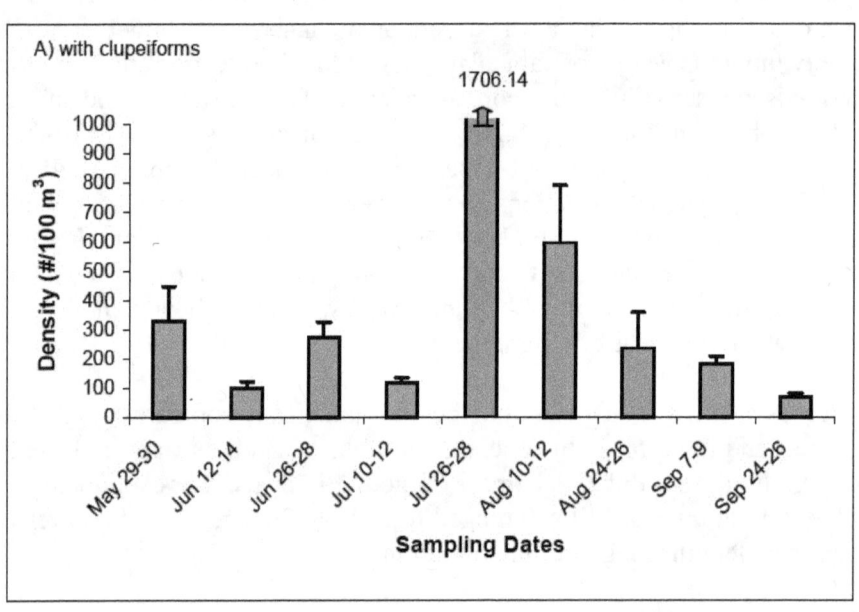

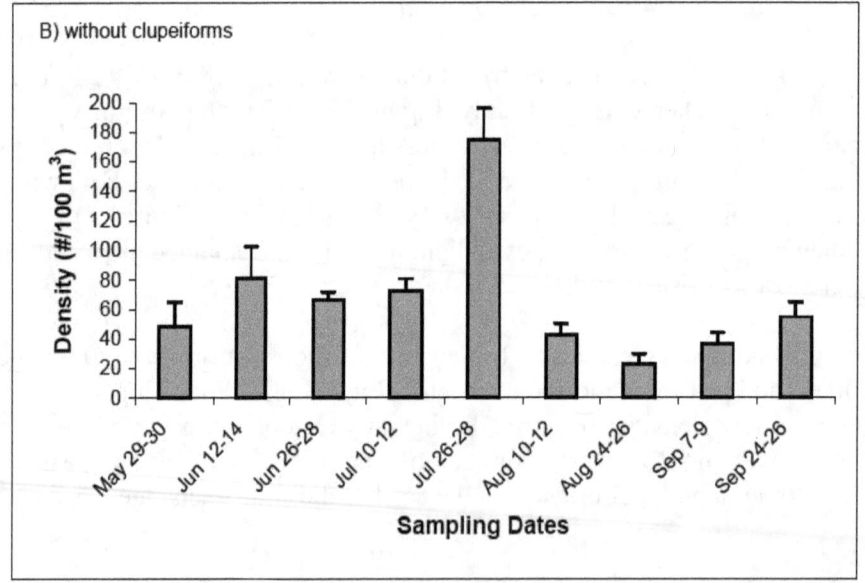

Figure 16. Mean plankton net densities (with standard errors) by sampling trip at the outer shelf platform MP 259 (1999) for data a) with clupeiforms and b) without clupeiforms included. Arrow above the bar points to the mean for that trip.

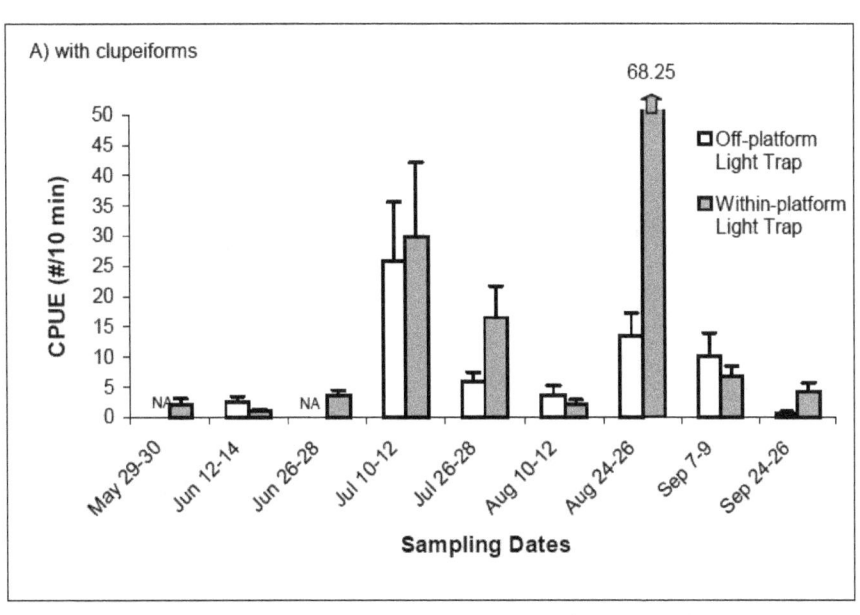

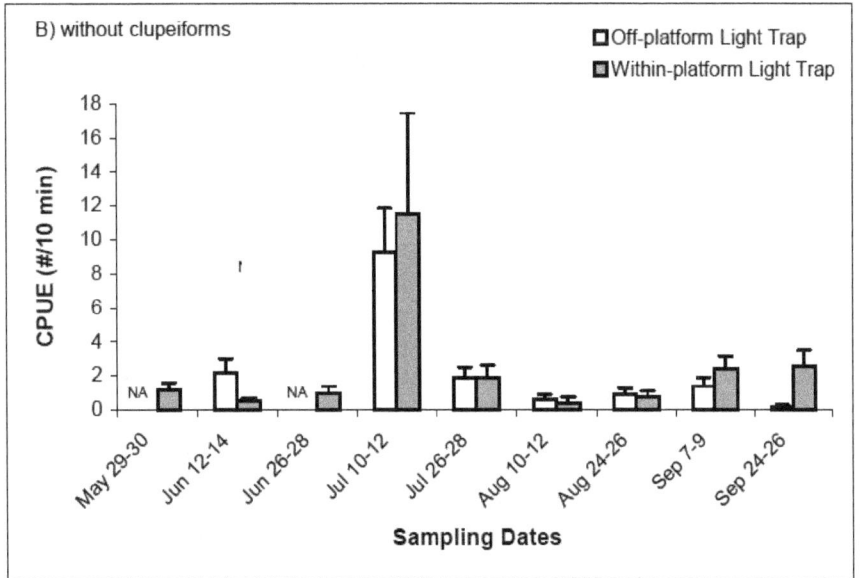

Figure 17. Mean light trap CPUEs (with standard errors) by sampling trip at the outer shelf platform MP 259 (1999) for data a) with clupeiforms and b) without clupeiforms included. NA = data not collected due to deployment problems. Arrow above the bar points to the mean for that gear.

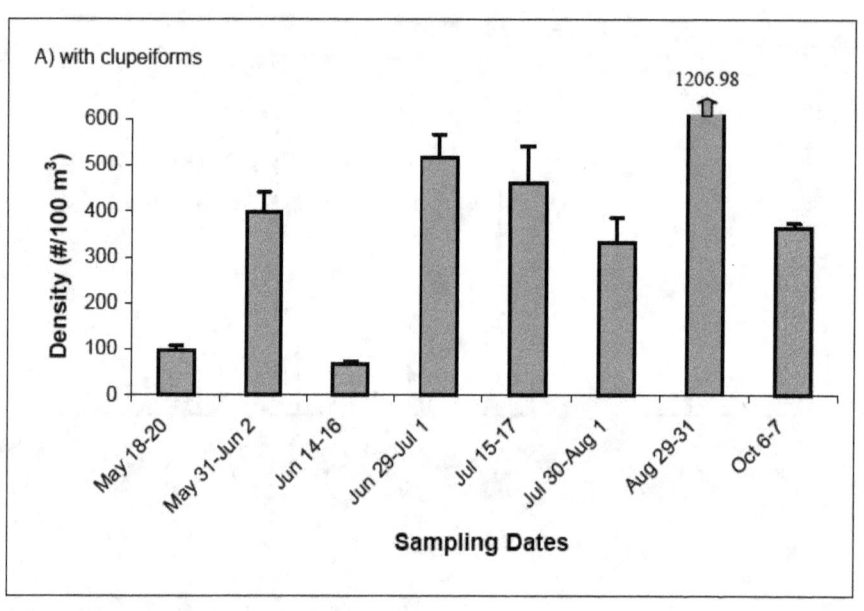

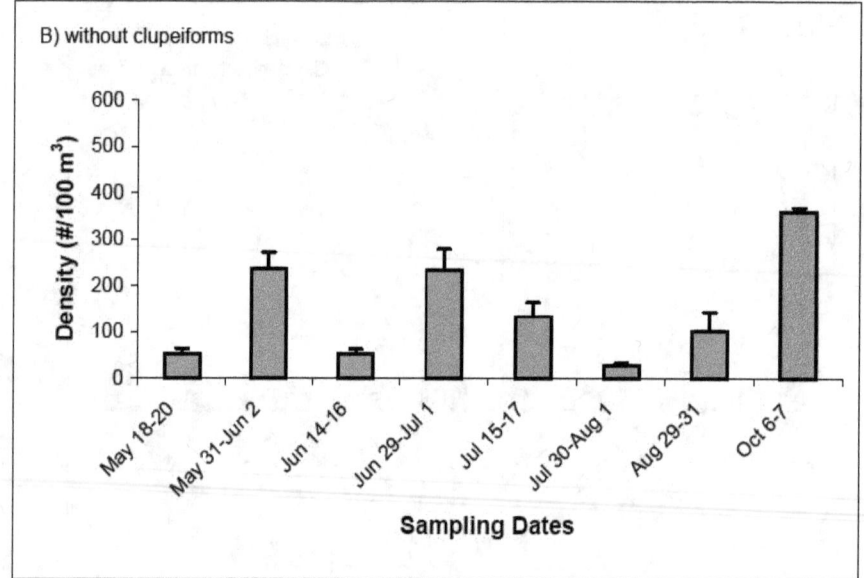

Figure 18. Mean plankton net densities (with standard errors) by sampling trip at the mid-shelf platform VK 203 (2000) for data a) with clupeiforms and b) without clupeiforms included. Arrow above the bar points to the mean for that trip.

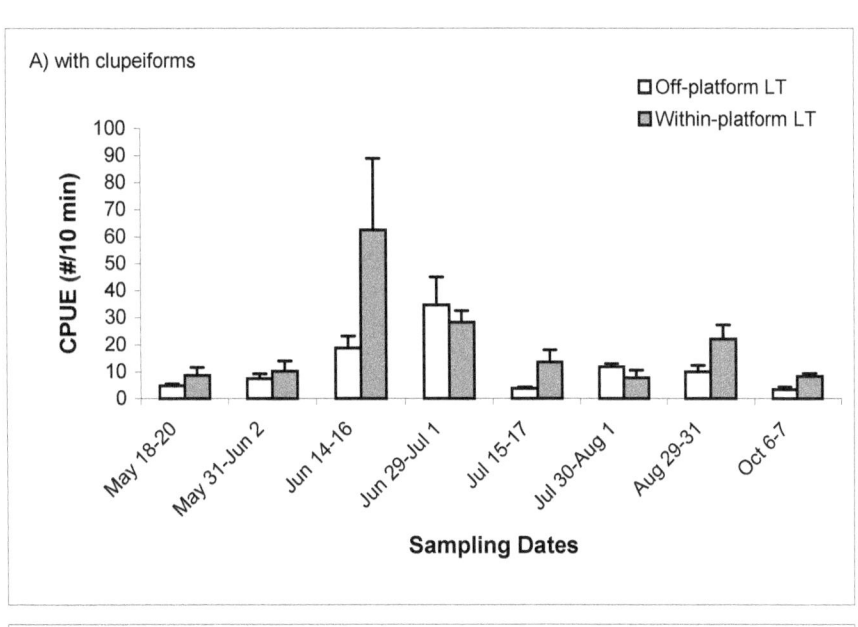

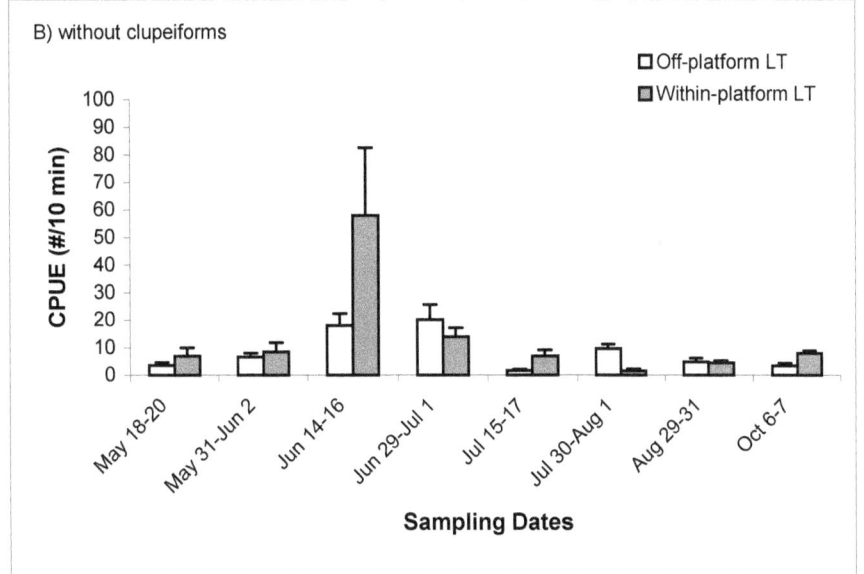

Figure 19. Mean light trap CPUEs (with standard errors) by sampling trip at the mid-shelf platform VK 203 (2000) for data a) with clupeiforms and b) without clupeiforms included

57

MP 259

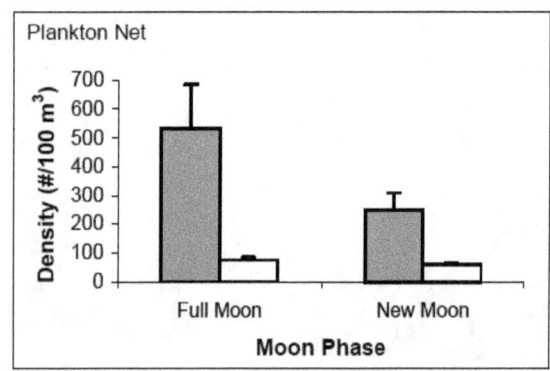

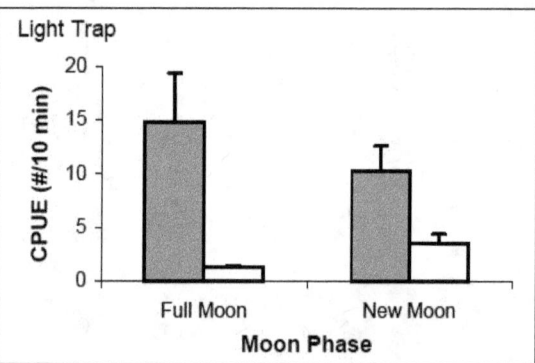

VK 203

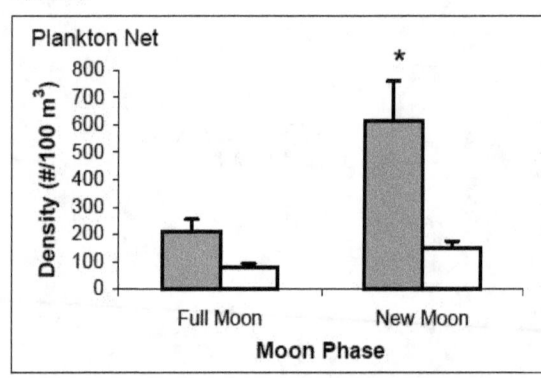

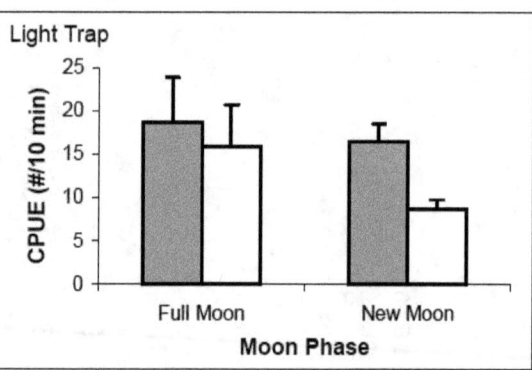

Figure 20. Mean plankton net densities and light trap CPUEs (with standard errors) for lunar phases sampled at MP 259 and VK 203 for data with clupeiforms (shaded bars) and without clupeiforms included (open bars). Asterisk denotes significant differences between lunar phases using the Wilcoxon 2-sample test.

were significantly higher during new moons than full moons (Wilcoxon Z = -2.46, p<0.02; Figure 20). When clupeiforms were removed, mean densities were still higher during new moons, though not significantly. Mean total light trap CPUEs were relatively equal between full and new moons, however, catch rates were slightly higher during full moons. When clupeiforms were excluded, this difference was somewhat larger.

Preflexion reef fish larvae were found in higher frequencies during either new or full moons, depending on the taxa, while postflexion larvae were collected almost exclusively during new moons (Table 15). Preflexion unidentified blenniids and *Hypsoblennius hentz/ionthas* had significantly higher frequencies collected during full moons. Preflexion holocentrids and labrids were also collected more frequently during full moons. In contrast, preflexion lutjanids, serranids, and other blenniids such as *Hypsoblennius invemar* and *Scartella/Hypleurochilus* were taken more frequently during new moons, while the pomacentrid *Chromis* spp. was only collected on new moons. Postflexion blenniids (*H. hentz/ionthas*, *H. invemar*, *Parablennius marmoreus*, and *Scartella/Hypleurochilus*), lutjanids (*Lutjanus* spp. and *Rhomboplites aurorubens*), pomacentrids (*Chromis* spp. and *Pomacentrus* spp.), and holocentrids were collected in significantly higher frequencies during new moons. Other postflexion taxa, such as labrids, scarids, epinephelines and serranines, were generally low in number, but were still collected in higher frequencies during new moons. *Lutjanus campechanus* was the only postflexion taxon that was collected in significantly higher frequencies during full moons.

Among Trip and Night Variability in Plankton Net and Light Trap Catches

Variability among the mean plankton net and light trap catches per night was consistently greater than among the mean plankton net and light trap catches per trip for each taxon at the mid-shelf platform GI 94 (Table 16). The taxa with the highest coefficients of variation (CVs) exhibited discrete pulses, spanning one to two nights, in their nightly mean densities or CPUEs. These pulses accounted for a high percentage of the total number of a taxon collected by a gear. For example, *Auxis* spp. and *Cynoscion arenarius* had among the highest CVs (both trip and night) and exhibited large pulses that accounted for 68% and 52%, respectively, of their total numbers collected by plankton nets (Figure 21). In contrast, plankton net-collected Serranidae and *Bregmaceros cantori* did not exhibit as discrete a pulse, were generally more common throughout the sampling season, and consequently had lower CVs. Light trap-collected *Hypsoblennius invemar* and Pomacentridae had high CVs and exhibited noticeable pulses over one to two nights that accounted for 43% and 65%, respectively, of their total catches. *Saurida brasiliensis* and Lutjanidae had relatively low CVs and though peak catches were observed they were not as distinct.

Coefficients of variation (CVs) for taxa collected at the mid-shelf platform VK 203 were generally lower than at GI 94, and displayed smaller differences between CVs among nights and among trips (Table 17). However, variability among nights remained slightly higher than the variability among trips in nearly all situations, and in the few exceptions the CVs were nearly equal. Despite this, distinct pulses were still evident. Large single pulses were observed for both *Saurida brasiliensis* (73% of the total catch) and *Synodus foetens* (65%) collected in light traps. As at GI 94, light trap-collected *Hypsoblennius invemar* at VK 203 exhibited a discrete pulse in nightly mean CPUEs spanning one night, however, a second smaller pulse occurred two trips

Table 15. Total numbers of pre- and postflexion reef larvae collected on new and full moons at all platforms combined (except GC18 where sampling only occurred on new moons). Asterisk denotes significant differences between moon phases using the chi-square goodness of fit test (p<0.01).

Reef Taxa	Preflexion			Postflexion		
	Full Moon		New Moon	Full Moon		New Moon
Blenniidae						
Unidentified	205	*	119	0		1
Hypsoblennius hentz/ionthas	10	*	1	16	*	63
Hypsoblennius invemar	1		12	32	*	734
Parablennius marmroeus	3		0	21	*	622
Scartella/Hypleurochilus	12		21	28	*	147
Holocentridae	8		1	1	*	15
Labridae	6		0	0		2
Lutjanidae						
Lutjanus campechanus	4		6	16	*	2
Lutjanus spp.	15		26	1	*	22
Pristipomoides aquilonaris	3		1	1		0
Rhomboplites aurorubens	1		4	7	*	48
Pomacentridae						
Abudefduf saxatilis	0		0	0		9
Chromis spp.	0	*	16	0	*	12
Pomacentrus spp.	1		2	11	*	86
Scaridae	0		2	0		3
Serranidae						
Anthinae	7		12	0		1
Epinephelinae	2		3	1		6
Grammistinae	3		1	1		1
Serraninae	11		16	1		7

Table 16. Coefficients of variation of the mean densities and CPUEs by sampling trip and sampling night for the ten most abundant taxa taken by plankton nets and light traps, and reef families collected at the mid-shelf platform GI 94.

	Plankton Net		Light Trap	
	Trip	Night	Trip	Night
Dominant Taxa				
Auxis spp.	237.7	347.5	206.7	245.4
Bregmaceros cantori	89.0	134.1	.	.
Cynoscion arenarius	292.7	420.7	.	.
Etropus crossotus	88.9	146.8	.	.
Euthynnus alletteratus	171.4	207.2	151.3	191.8
Gobiidae	46.8	78.2	.	.
Hypsoblennius invemar	.	.	202.3	245.1
Hypsoblennius hentz/ionthas	.	.	268.2	325.4
Parablennius marmoreus	.	.	135.8	164.0
Peprilus paru	322.2	457.0	.	.
Saurida brasiliensis	144.6	150.6	91.2	115.4
Scomberomorus cavalla	.	.	207.1	258.7
Scomberomorus maculatus	.	.	162.2	214.8
Symphurus spp.	132.2	138.9	.	.
Synodus foetens	228.2	243.7	205.7	224.1
Synodus poeyi	.	.	124.0	155.9
Reef Families				
Lutjanidae	131.1	179.5	173.5	221.9
Pomacentridae	292.7	432.9	221.4	231.8
Serranidae	99.8	159.3	196.3	224.2

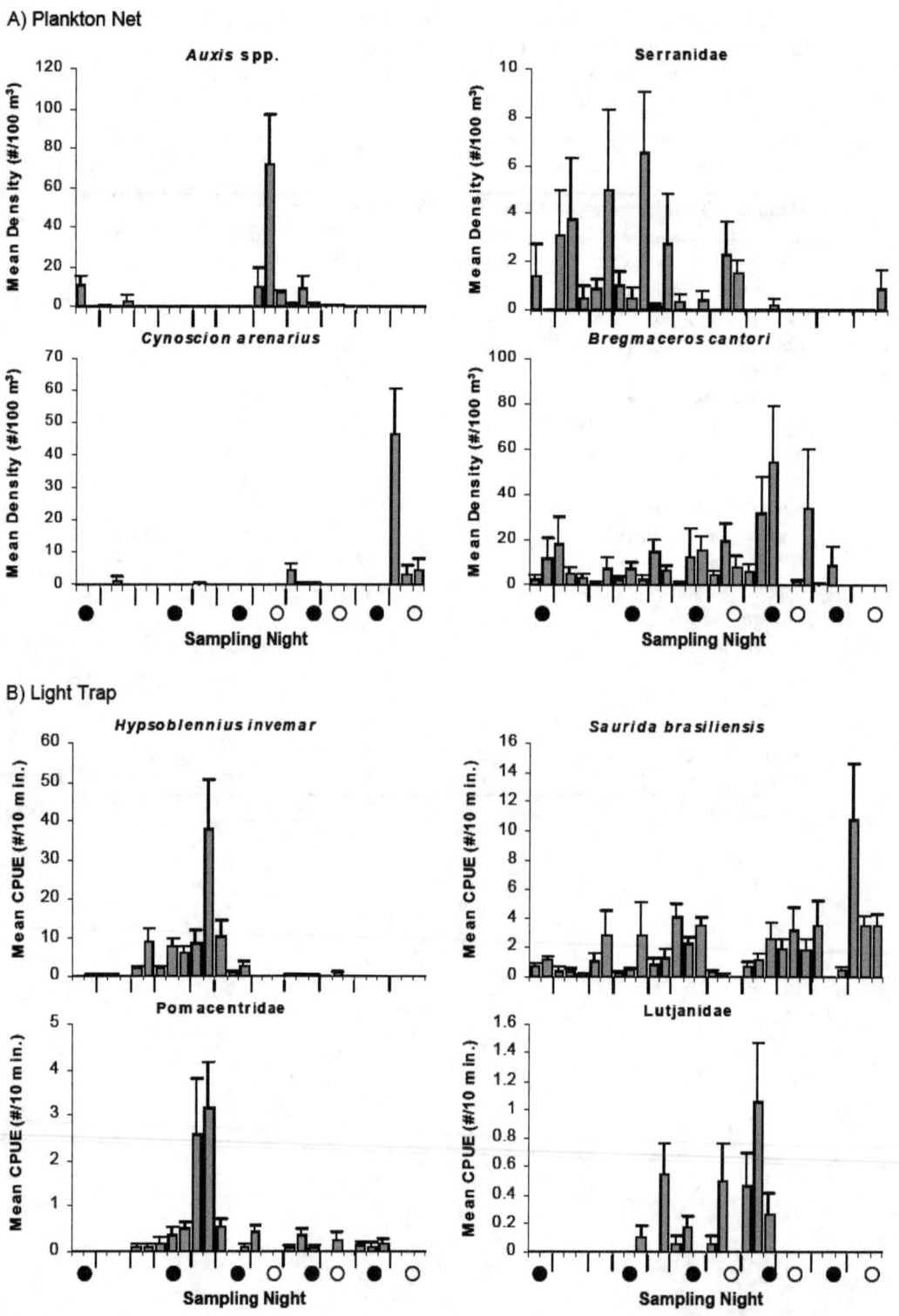

Figure 21. Mean plankton net densities and light trap CPUEs (with standard errors) by sampling night for fish taxa collected at GI 94. Longer tick marks on x-axis delimit sampling trips. Open circles represent full moons, and dark circles represent new moons. The second and fifth sampling trips occurred during first quarter moons, while the third sampling trip occurred during a last quarter moon.

Table 17. Coefficients of variation of the mean densities and CPUEs by sampling trip and sampling night for the ten most abundant taxa taken by plankton nets and light traps, and reef families collected at the mid-shelf platform VK 203.

	Plankton Net		Light Trap	
	Trip	Night	Trip	Night
Dominant Taxa				
Auxis spp.	.	.	244.8	262.0
Bregmaceros cantori	202.1	228.2	.	.
Chloroscombrus chrysurus	194.8	192.9	.	.
Cynoscion arenarius	141.2	204.6	.	.
Decapterus punctatus	.	.	127.4	145.2
Eucinostomus spp.	.	.	133.5	178.4
Euthynnus alletteratus	.	.	225.6	264.8
Gobiidae	134.7	168.0	114.4	127.4
Hypsoblennius invemar	.	.	165.3	207.7
Microdesmus lanceolatus	121.5	118.9	.	.
Ophichthus spp.	178.9	176.1	.	.
Parablennius marmoreus	.	.	125.9	133.3
Saurida brasiliensis	196.4	186.3	217.1	279.0
Scartella/Hypleurochilus	116.0	154.7	.	.
Scomberomorus maculatus	179.0	247.4	129.1	183.3
Symphurus spp.	148.6	163.4	.	.
Synodus foetens	.	.	169.1	243.1
Reef Families				
Lutjanidae	123.2	160.4	103.4	152.8
Pomacentridae	.	.	179.3	166.9
Serranidae	92.2	115.0	151.2	222.6

63

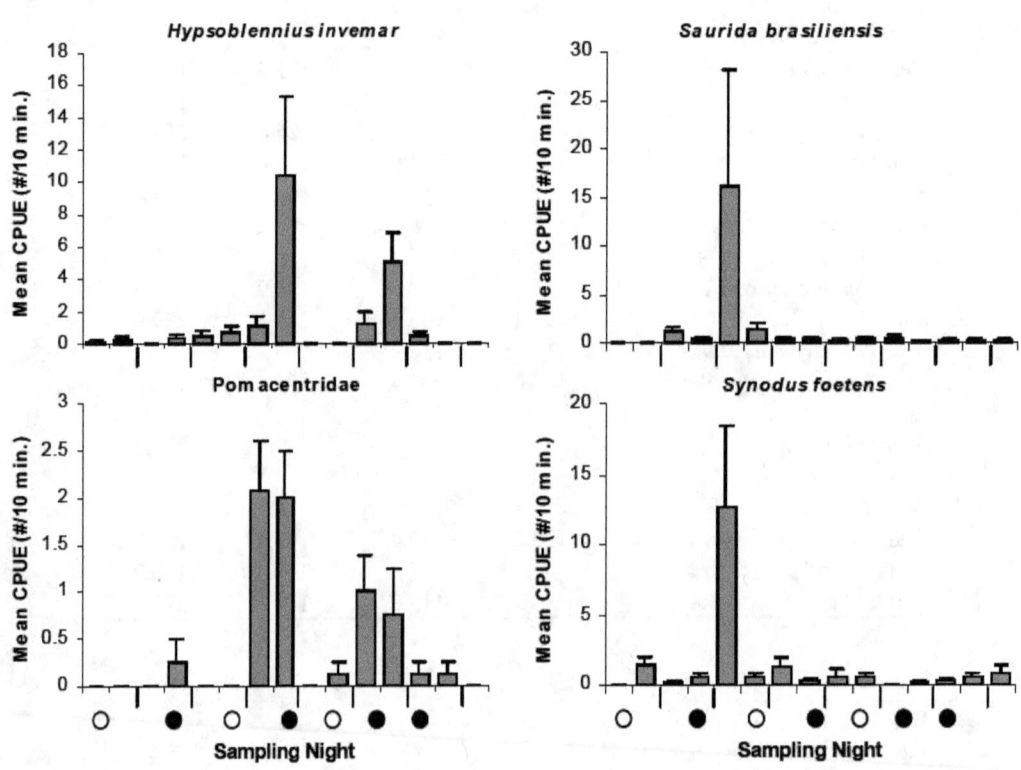

Figure 22. Mean light trap CPUEs (with standard errors) by sampling night for fish taxa collected at VK 203. Longer tick marks on x-axis delimit sampling trips. Open circles represent full moons, and dark circles represent new moons. The last sampling trip occurred during a first quarter moon.

later (two pulses combined = 88% of the total catch; Figure 22). Although it was the only taxa collected by light traps to have a CV higher among trips than among nights, Pomacentridae at VK 203 still exhibited two discrete pulses (combined = 90% of the total catch).

Pulses were also observed to coincide among taxa, particularly in light trap collections. At GI 94, the pulses of *Hypsoblennius invemar* and Pomacentridae (which itself consisted of both *Pomacentrus* spp. and *Chromis* spp.) both occurred over the same one to two night span during the fifth sampling trip (Figure 21). Similarly, at VK 203 *H. invemar* and Pomacentridae had pulses that coincided during both the fourth and sixth sampling trips, which both occurred during new moon phases (Figure 22). Furthermore, pulses of the synodontids *Saurida brasiliensis* and *Synodus foetens* coincided during the third sampling trip. A similar multi-taxa pulse occurred during the fourth sampling trip at MP 259, when 100% of the *H. invemar* and Pomacentridae catch, and greater than 95% of the *Holocentrus* spp. and *Synodus foetens* total catch was taken.

Within-Night Variability in Plankton Net and Light Trap Catches

Mean total plankton net and light trap catches by within-night time of capture (averaged across all sampling trips at each platform) were considerably variable, and no consistent patterns were observed among platforms (Figure 23). Peaks in mean plankton net densities ranged from four hours after sunset at ST 54 to ten hours at GI 94. The within-night variability in plankton net densities mostly reflected episodic catches of clupeiform larvae. When clupeiforms were removed, variability was reduced and the mean densities were surprisingly uniform throughout the night at each platform, with the exception of GC 18 where non-clupeiform densities peaked during the middle of the night. There were no significant differences in mean densities by hours sampled after sunset at any of the platforms. Light trap catches at ST 54 and MP 259 peaked about 3-4 hours after sunset and gradually declined thereafter, while at other platforms CPUEs peaked later in the night (VK 203: 5-6 hours; GI 94 and GC 18: 8 hours). As in plankton nets, the within-night variability in light trap CPUEs was largely attributable to clupeiforms. There were no significant differences in mean CPUEs by hour after sunset, except at GC 18 (χ^2 = 45.68, p<0.0001, with clupeiforms; χ^2 = 41.50, p<0.0001, without clupeiforms). Attempts were made to estimate the within-night variability of the dominant taxa and reef families, however, mean densities and CPUEs were extremely variable and no notable patterns were observed.

Length-Frequency and Developmental Stages of Reef Taxa

Blenniids were the most abundant reef-associated taxa collected at platforms, and were represented by a wide range of sizes and developmental stages. At the inner shelf platform ST 54, most of blenniids were postflexion and settlement size *Hypsoblennius invemar*, *H. hentz/ionthas* and *Scartella/Hypleurochilus* between 9 and 13 mm (Figure 24). A large number of recently-hatched and preflexion unidentified blenniids were also collected. The most common blenniids collected at the mid-shelf platform VK 203 were postflexion/settlement size *H. invemar* 10 to 12 mm in length. A wide range of *Scartella/Hypleurochilus*, from recently-hatched to settlement size, were also collected at VK 203. Blenniids were most numerous at GI 94 and were dominated by *H. invemar* and *Parablennius marmoreus*, representing preflexion larvae of 4 to 5 mm up to postflexion/settlement larvae of 23 mm. Flexion and postflexion *H.*

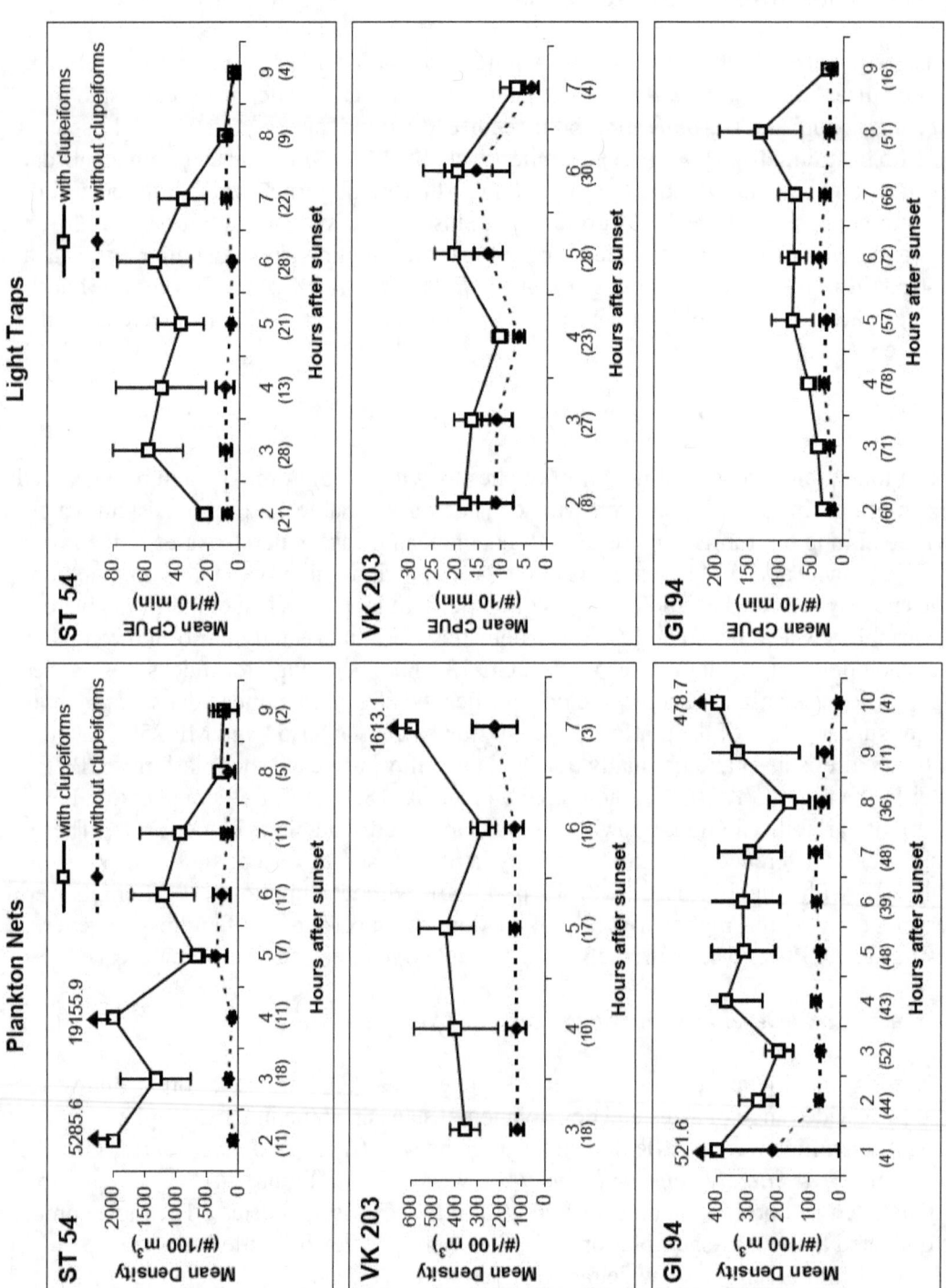

Figure 23. Mean plankton net densities and light trap CPUEs (with standard errors) by number of hours after sunset that collections were taken in surface waters at each platform, for data with and without clupeiforms included. Arrows above the symbols point to the mean for that hour. Numbers in parentheses indicate the number of samples for each hour.

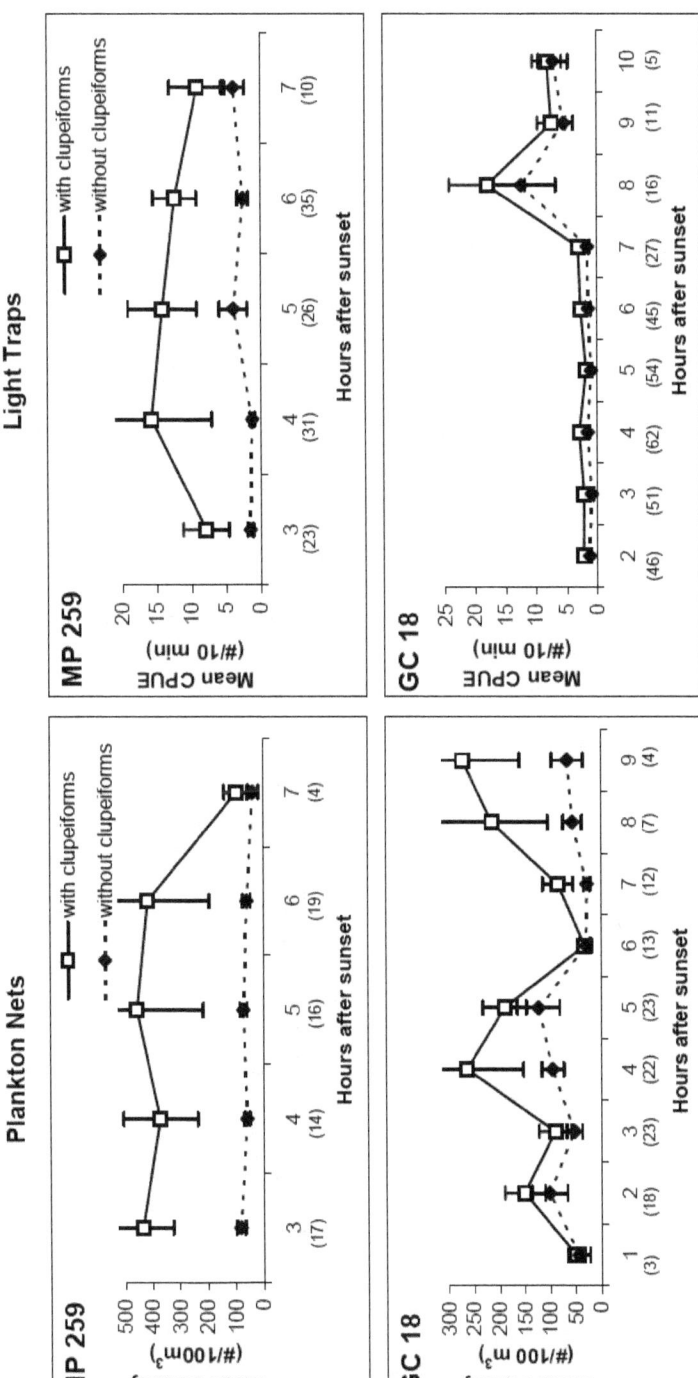

Figure 23. (continued)

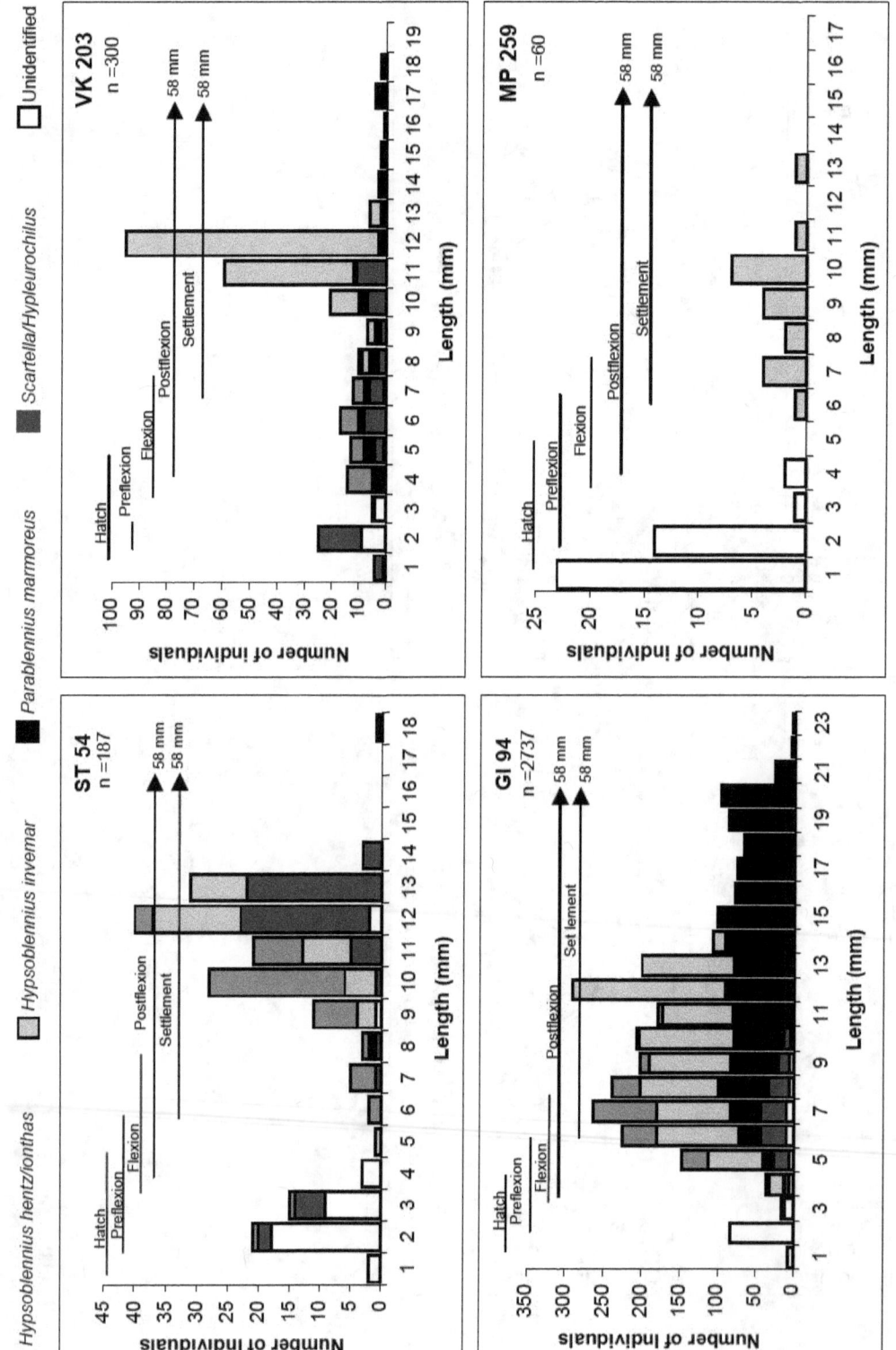

Figure 24. Size distributions of blenniids collected at each platform. Lines above the bars denote the size ranges of different early life history stages based on published literature. n = total number of fishes measured.

68

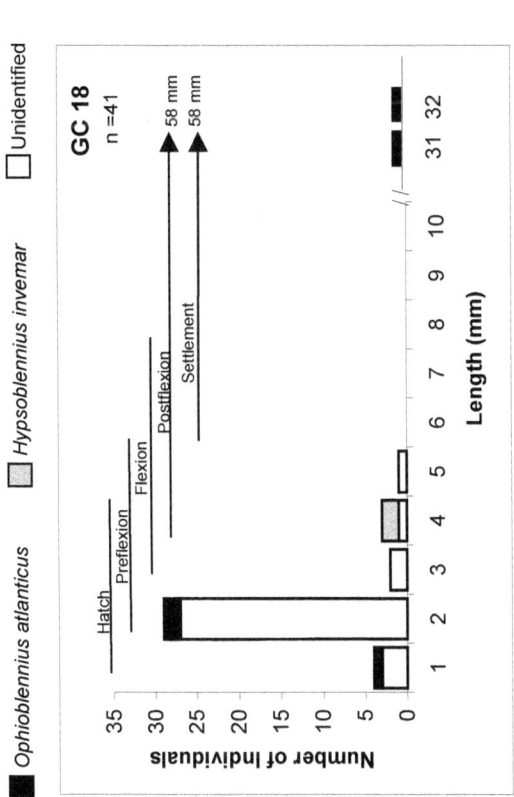

Figure 24. (continued)

69

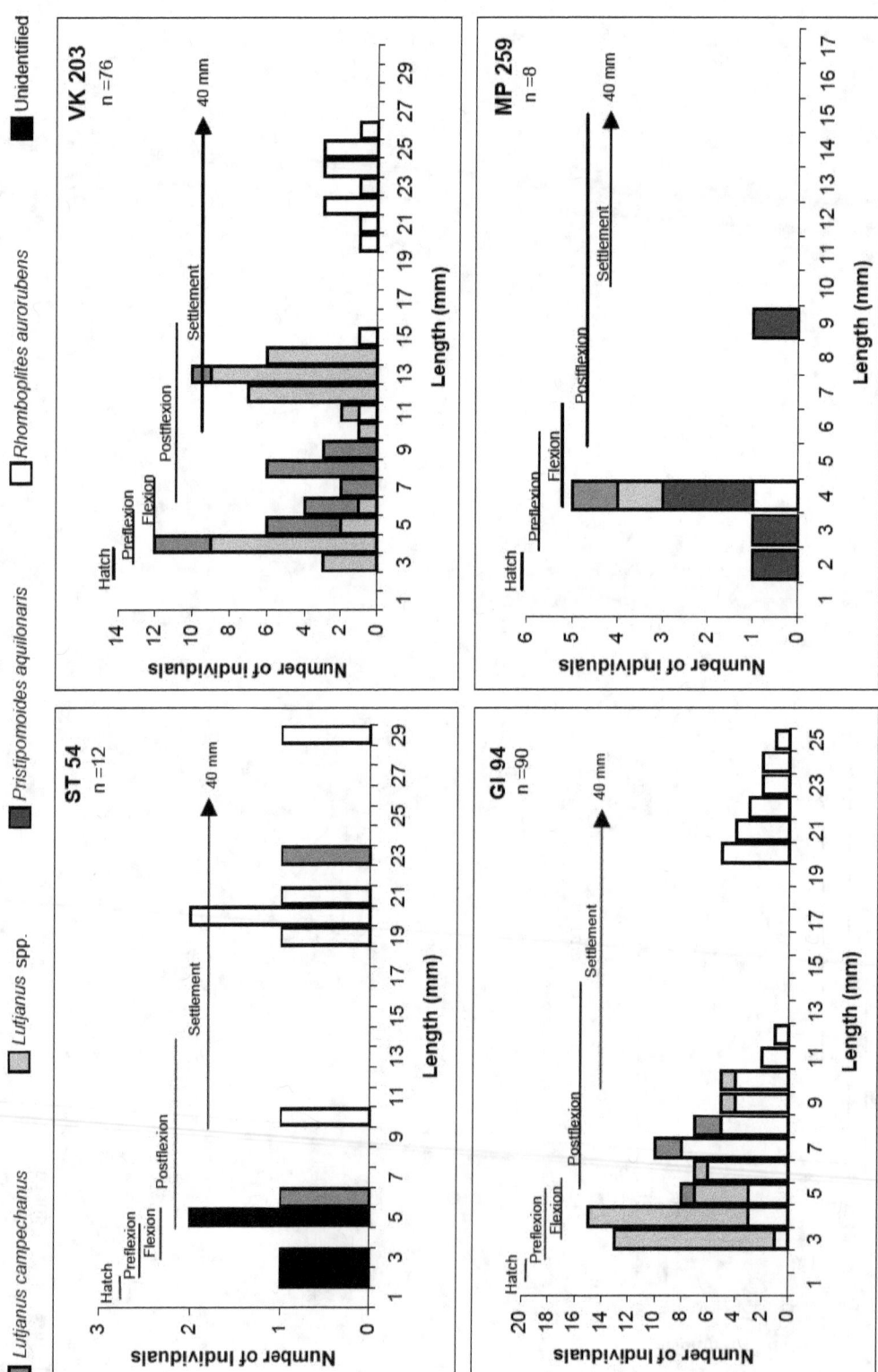

Figure 25. Size distributions of lutjanids collected at each platform. Lines above the bars denote the size ranges of different early life history stages based on published literature. n = total number of fishes measured.

70

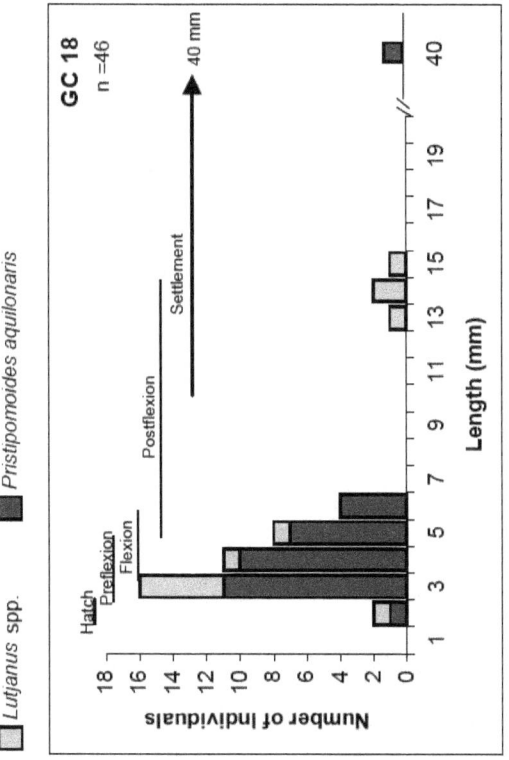

Figure 25. (continued)

71

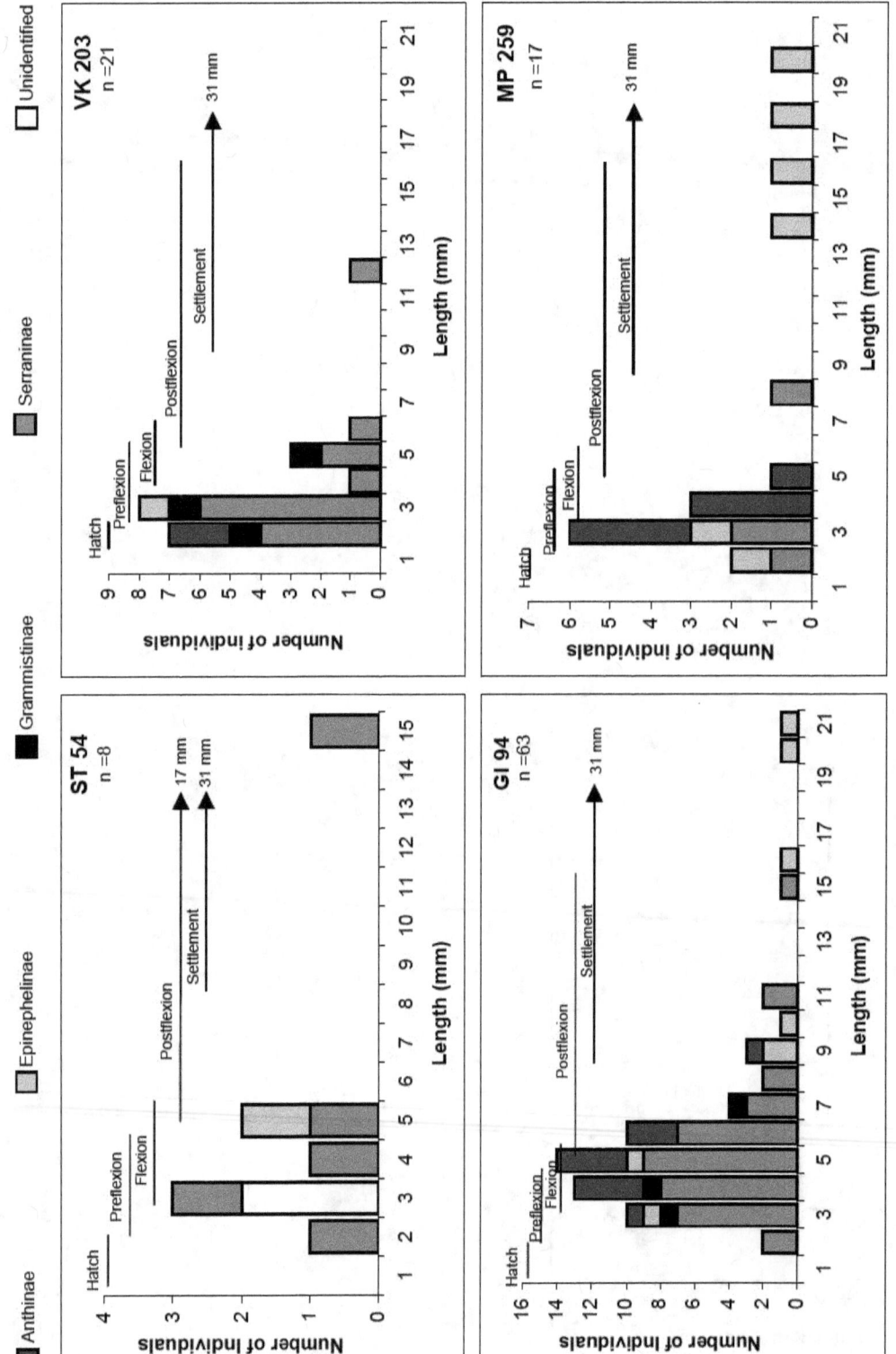

Figure 26. Size distributions of serranids collected at each platform. Lines above the bars denote the size ranges of different early life history stages based on published literature. n = total number of fishes measured.

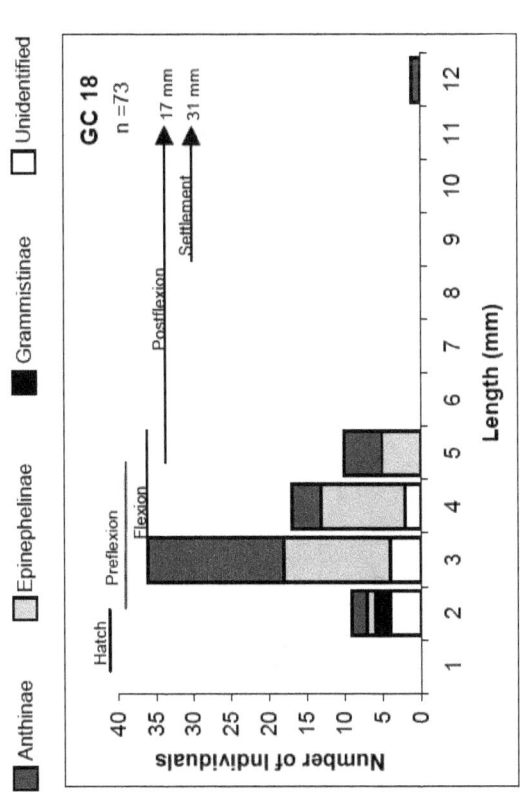

Figure 26. (continued)

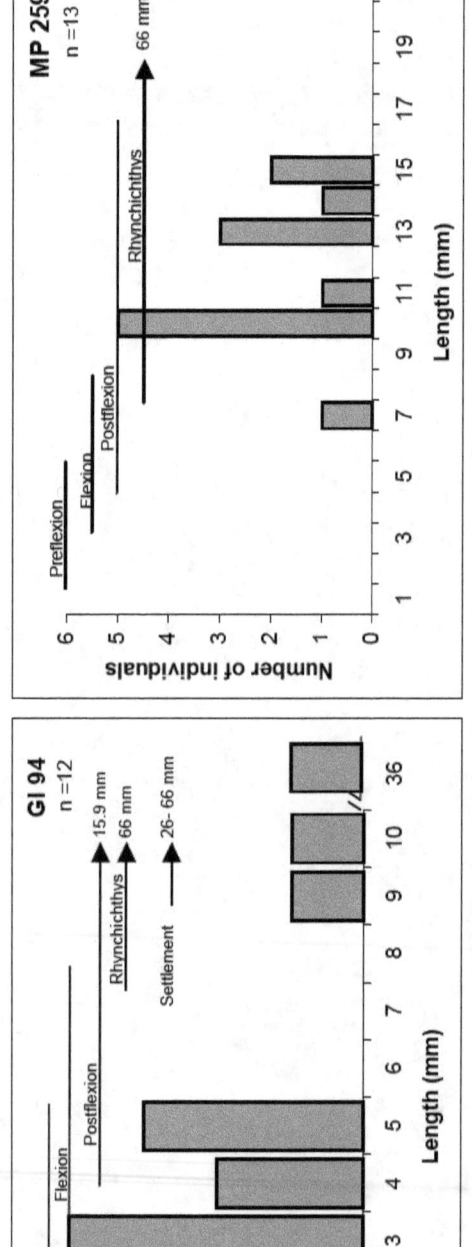

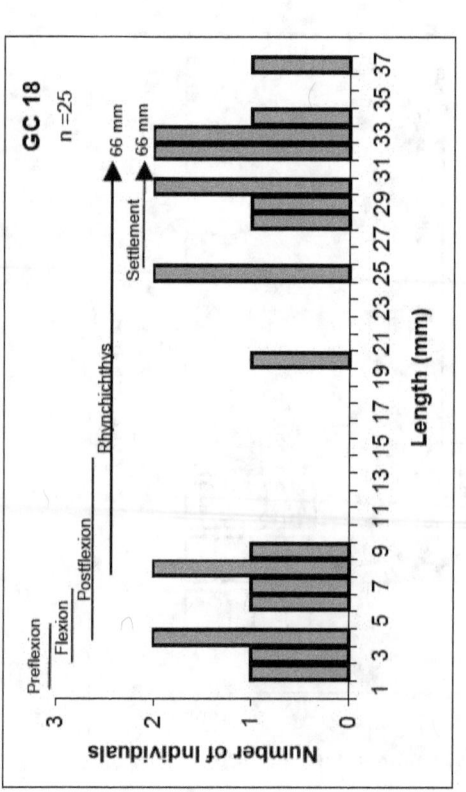

Figure 27. Size distributions of holocentrids collected at each platform. Lines above the bars denote the size ranges of different early life history stages based on published literature. n = total number of fishes measured.

74

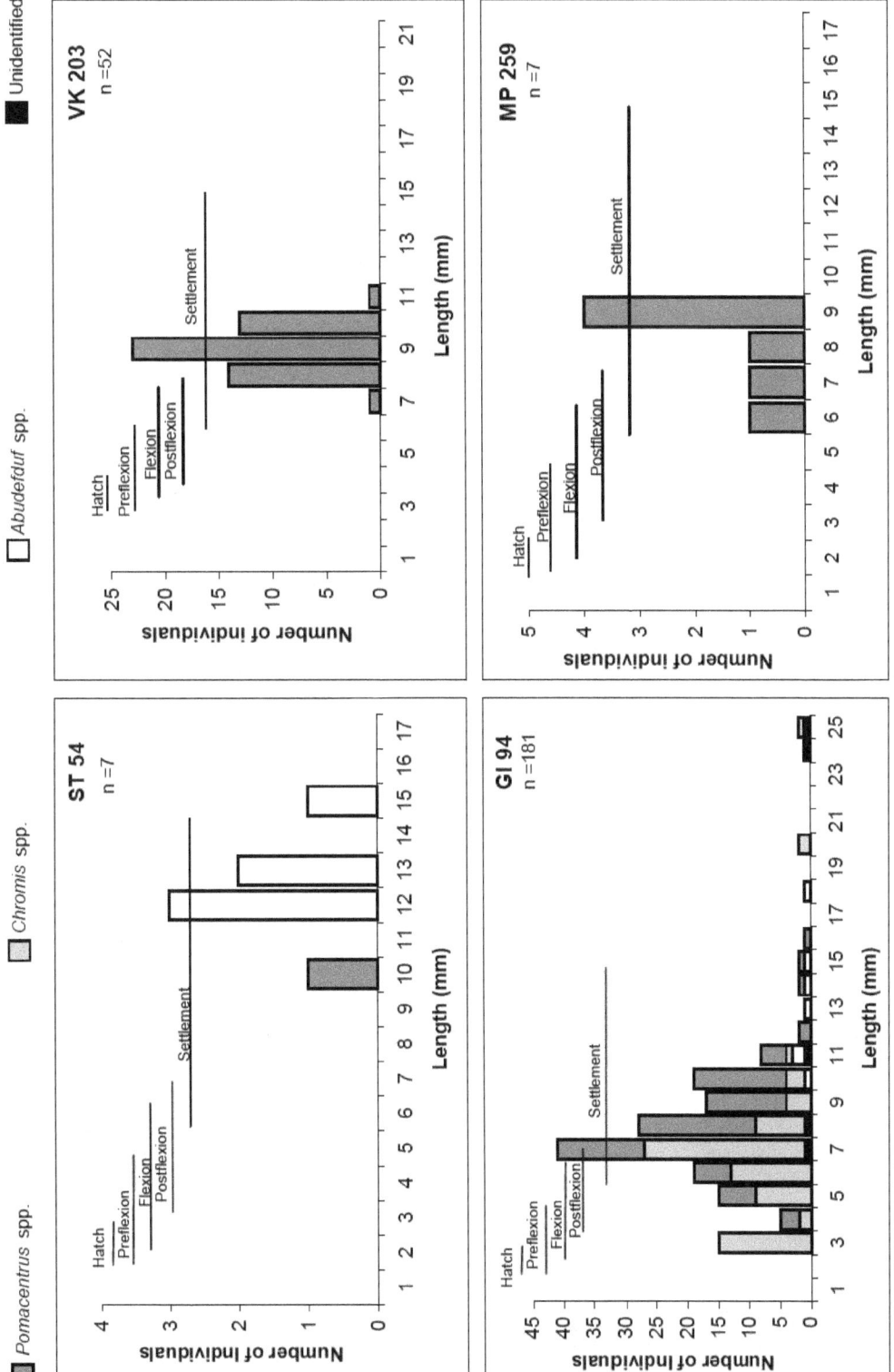

Figure 28. Size distributions of pomacentrids collected at each platform. Lines above the bars denote the size ranges of different early life history stages based on published literature. n = total number of fishes measured.

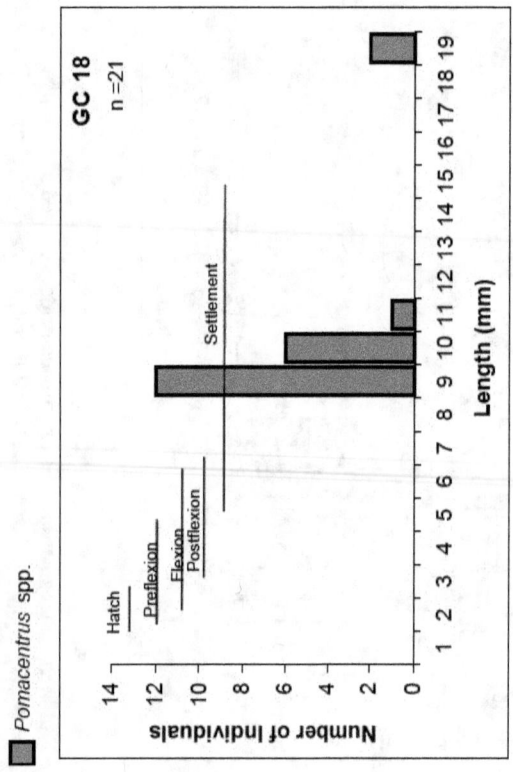

Figure 28. (continued)

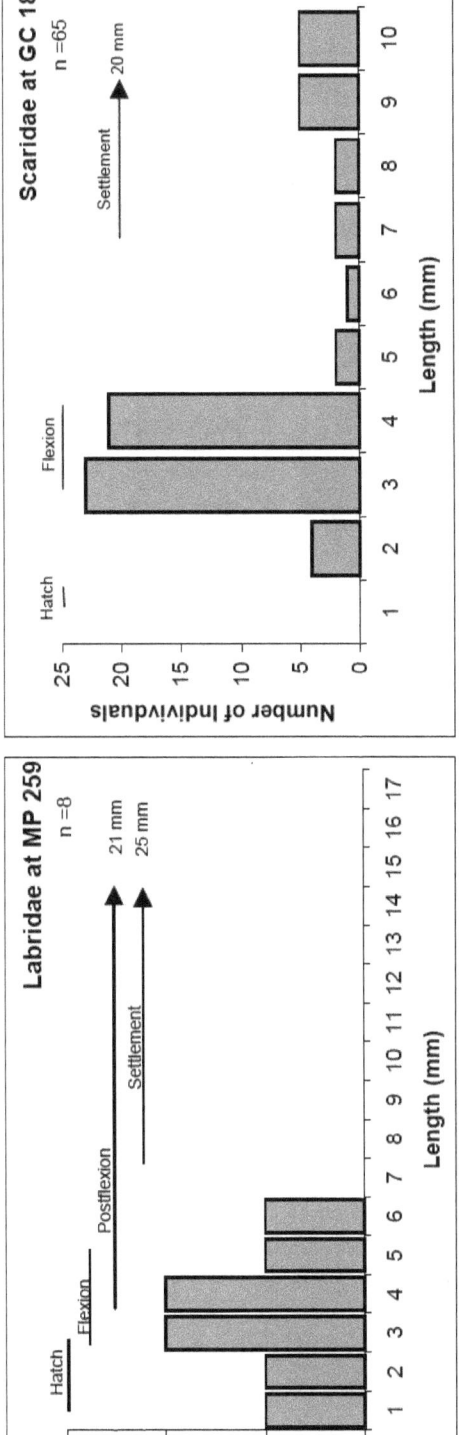

Figure 29. Size distributions of labrids collected at MP 259 and scarids collected at GC 18. Lines above the bars denote the size ranges of different early life history stages based on published literature. n = total number of fishes measured.

77

hentz/ionthas, and recently-hatched unidentified blenniids were also common at GI 94. Fewer numbers of blenniids were taken at the outer shelf platforms, MP 259 and GC 18, and these were predominantly recently-hatched unidentified blenniids. However, a small number of postflexion and settlement size *H. invemar* were taken at MP 259, and two postflexion/settlement *Ophioblennius atlanticus* were taken at GC 18.

Lutjanids were also collected in a wide range of sizes and developmental stages; however, most were preflexion and flexion larvae <7 mm in length (Figure 25). Very few lutjanids (n = 12) were collected at the inner shelf platform ST 54, and most were settlement size *Rhomboplites aurorubens* between 19 to 29 mm in length. Settlement size *Lutjanus* spp. (12-14 mm in length) and *R. aurorubens* (20-26 mm) were common at the mid-shelf platform VK 203. A relatively large number of pre- to postflexion *Lutjanus* spp. and *L. campechanus* were also collected at VK 203. Lutjanids at GI 94 were represented by pre- to post flexion *Lutjanus* spp. and *L. campechanus*, and two size groups of *R. aurorubens* (3-12 mm pre- to postflexion larvae and 20-25 mm settlement size juveniles). Most of lutjanids collected at the outer shelf platforms, MP 259 and GC 18, were pre- to postflexion *Pristipomoides aquilonaris*; however, a small number of settlement size *Lutjanus* spp. and a 40-mm *P. aquilonaris* were collected at GC 18.

Serranids collected at platforms were almost exclusively pre- to postflexion larvae between 2 to 6 mm in length (Figure 26). Larger settlement size serranids were rare and included: single specimens of Serraninae at ST 54 and VK 203 (15 and 12 mm in length, respectively), a number of serranines and epinephelines at GI 94 and MP 259 (9-21 mm), and a single anthiine collected at GC 18 (12 mm).

While relatively few in number, holocentrids collected at platforms were represented by several developmental stages (Figure 27). At the mid-shelf platform GI 94, most holocentrids were preflexion to postflexion larvae between 3 and 5 mm in length, however three postflexion/rhynchichthys larvae were also collected. The holocentrids collected at the outer shelf platform MP 259 were generally postflexion/rhynchichthys larvae. At GC 18, two groups of holocentrids were collected: preflexion to postflexion larvae 2 to 9 mm in length, and rhynchichthys/settlement size larvae 20 to 37 mm in length.

Pomacentrids were the most abundant reef-dependent taxa collected at platforms, and were predominantly collected as settlement size juveniles 7 to 15 mm in length (Figure 28). Most of these juveniles were *Pomacentrus* spp., however, a small number of *Abudefduf* spp. were collected at ST 54 and GI 94, and *Chromis* spp. were common at GI 94. Preflexion to postflexion *Chromis* spp. and *Pomacentrus* spp. larvae were also abundant at GI 94.

Larvae of other reef-dependent taxa were relatively rare at platforms, and of those collected most were recently-hatched to postflexion larvae. A small number of labrids were collected at MP 259, ranging from 1 to 6 mm in length (Figure 29). Scarids were most numerous at the GC 18, and were represented by preflexion to settlement size larvae (Figure 29). Four scarids 5 to 6 mm in length were also taken at MP 259. The only other reef-dependent taxa collected at platforms were single 4-mm chaetodontids collected at GI 94 and GC 18.

Environmental Variables and Larval and Juvenile Fish Abundances

Salinity, temperature, turbidity, and microzooplankton biomass all were influential in describing trends in the abundances of the top 15 dominant taxa and reef fish families at the outer shelf platform MP 259. For plankton net collections, densities of *Auxis* spp., *Euthynnus alletteratus* and *Symphurus* spp. were positively associated with the first environmental canonical variate, which was primarily influenced by temperature (Table 18). *Bregmaceros cantori* and Myctophidae were negatively associated with the first environmental variate. Densities of *Scomberomorus maculatus* were positively associated with the second environmental variate, which was positively influenced by turbidity and microzooplankton biomass. Myctophidae and Serranidae densities were positively associated with the third environmental variate, which was positively correlated with salinity and negatively correlated with temperature and turbidity. Within light trap collections, *Decapterus punctatus*, *Holocentrus* spp., *Hypsoblennius invemar*, *Pomacentrus* spp., and *Synodus foetens* were positively associated with the first environmental variate, which was positively correlated with salinity and negatively correlated with turbidity and microzooplankton biomass (Table 19). *Chloroscombrus chrysurus* was negatively associated with the second environmental variate, which was positively correlated with salinity and negatively correlated with temperature.

Salinity and microzooplankton biomass were the most influential environmental variables in describing trends in larval and juvenile fish abundance at the mid-shelf platform VK 203. In plankton net collections, densities of *Microdesmus lanceolatus* and *Sphyraena borealis* were negatively correlated with the first environmental canonical variate, which was positively influenced by salinity and microzooplankton biomass (Table 20). *Etropus crossotus* and Serranidae were positively associated and *Scartella/Hypleurochilus* was negatively associated with the second environmental, which was positively correlated with microzooplankton biomass and negatively correlated with temperature. *Bregmaceros cantori*, *E. crossotus*, *Saurida brasiliensis*, *Scomberomorus maculatus*, and *Symphurus* spp. were positively associated with the third environmental variate, which was positively correlated with suspended solids and microzooplankton biomass, and negatively correlated with salinity. For light trap collections, *Auxis* spp., *Caranx crysos* and *Euthynnus alletteratus* were positively associated, and *Hypsoblennius invemar* and *Pomacentrus* spp. were negatively associated with the first environmental variate, which was positively correlated with salinity (Table 21). *Scomberomorus maculatus* was positively associated, and *H. invemar*, *Pomacentrus* spp. and Lutjanidae were negatively associated with the second environmental variate, which was positively correlated with microzooplankton biomass.

Relationship Between Water Current Speed and Light Trap CPUE

Mean light trap CPUEs, from MP 259 and VK 203 combined, decreased with increasing water current speed (Figure 30). Highest mean light trap catches (>20 fish/10 min.) were at current speeds less than 30 cm s^{-1}, with or without clupeiforms included. CPUEs at current speeds above 30 cm s^{-1} were consistently less than 10 fish/10 min., although this observation is somewhat limited by the low number of samples at these current speeds.

Table 18. Results of a canonical correlation analysis on log-transformed plankton net densities (15 most abundant taxa, and reef fish families) and environmental variables for MP 259. Loadings in bold under statistically significant canonical variables V1, V2 and V3 explain at least 15% of the variation for that taxon. Loadings in bold under the environmental canonical variates W1, W2 and W3 indicate the most influential environmental variables. RA = reef associated taxa, RD = reef dependent taxa.

Canonical Correlation	Likelihood Ratio	Approximate F	Pr > F
1) 0.774921	0.08197861	1.8958	0.0002
2) 0.680626	0.20520408	1.6117	0.0117
3) 0.671726	0.38230996	1.5270	0.0514

Taxa	Correlations between plankton net densities and their canonical variates		
	V1	V2	V3
Auxis spp.	**0.5656**	0.0427	0.2794
Bothus spp.	-0.2224	0.0555	0.2860
Bregmaceros cantori	**-0.5841**	0.0437	0.3801
Caranx crysos	0.2056	-0.2525	-0.0471
Chloroscombrus chrysurus	0.0132	-0.2931	-0.1435
Cubiceps pauciradiatus	0.1655	0.0914	0.2145
Euthynnus alletteratus	**0.5891**	0.1888	0.2196
Gobiidae	-0.0724	-0.0855	0.0680
Labridae (RD)	-0.2339	-0.1597	0.0736
Lutjanidae (RA)	-0.2405	-0.1188	0.0540
Microdesmus lanceolatus	0.0701	0.3701	0.2202
Myctophidae	**-0.5082**	-0.0136	**0.4812**
Saurida brasiliensis	0.0517	-0.3211	0.2782
Scaridae (RD)	0.1807	0.2114	0.0040
Scomberomorus cavalla	0.0777	0.0855	0.2661
Scomberomorus maculatus	-0.1688	**0.5995**	-0.0356
Seriola spp.	-0.1831	0.1808	0.1269
Serranidae (RA)	-0.2921	-0.2370	**0.4581**
Symphurus spp.	**0.4941**	-0.0633	0.0672

Environmental Variables	Correlations between environmental variables and their canonical variates		
	W1	W2	W3
Surface Salinity	0.0801	-0.3369	**0.9343**
Surface Temperature	**0.5709**	-0.1679	**-0.7915**
Surface Turbidity	-0.0621	**0.8492**	**-0.4348**
Microzooplankton Biomass	0.3781	**0.6226**	-0.1321

Table 19. Results of a canonical correlation analysis on log-transformed light trap CPUEs (15 most abundant taxa) and environmental variables for MP 259. Loadings in bold under statistically significant canonical variables V1 and V2 explain at least 15% of the variation for that taxon. Loadings in bold under the environmental canonical variates W1 and W2 indicate the most influential environmental variables. RA= reef associated taxa, RD = reef dependent taxa.

Canonical Correlation	Likelihood Ratio	Approximate F	Pr > F
1) 0.575643	0.34934089	1.6434	0.0013
2) 0.507755	0.52246836	1.4006	0.0422

Taxa	Correlations between light trap CPUEs and their canonical variates	
	V1	V2
Auxis spp.	-0.0518	0.3702
Bregmaceros cantori	0.0312	0.2488
Caranx crysos	0.2316	-0.0651
Chloroscombrus chrysurus	-0.0856	**-0.6214**
Decapterus punctatus	**0.4450**	0.0627
Epinephelinae (RA)	0.1394	-0.1870
Euthynnus alletteratus	0.3537	-0.2673
Gobiidae	-0.0518	-0.2595
Holocentrus spp. (RA)	**0.6577**	0.0678
Hypsoblennius invemar (RA)	**0.4158**	0.0321
Myctophidae	-0.1813	0.2465
Pomacentrus spp. (RD)	**0.3872**	0.0554
Saurida brasiliensis	0.0906	-0.2457
Scomberomorus maculatus	-0.0967	0.1340
Synodus foetens	**0.4239**	0.0134

Environmental Variables	Correlations between environmental variables and their canonical variates	
	W1	W2
Surface Salinity	**0.6789**	**0.6435**
Surface Temperature	-0.0958	**-0.9602**
Surface Turbidity	**-0.6706**	-0.0270
Microzooplankton Biomass	**-0.4754**	-0.2961

Table 20. Results of the canonical correlation analysis on log-transformed plankton net densities (15 most abundant taxa, and reef fish families) and environmental variables for VK 203. Loadings in bold under statistically significant canonical variables V1, V2 and V3 explain at least 15% of the variation for that taxon. Loadings in bold under the environmental canonical variates W1, W2 and W3 indicate the most influential environmental variables. RA = reef associated taxa.

Canonical Correlation	Likelihood Ratio	Approximate F	Pr > F
1) 0.819470	0.03894454	3.1261	0.0001
2) 0.777732	0.11856371	2.7905	0.0001
3) 0.753257	0.30005993	2.4177	0.0011

Taxa	Correlations between plankton net densities and their canonical variates		
	V1	V2	V3
Bregmaceros cantori	-0.0151	0.3816	**0.4228**
Caranx crysos	0.2905	-0.0590	-0.2477
Chloroscombrus chrysurus	-0.2691	0.3119	0.2830
Cynoscion arenarius	0.0670	0.0950	0.0020
Etropus crossotus	0.0170	**0.3880**	**0.4254**
Gobiidae	-0.2605	0.0293	0.2109
Lutjanidae (RA)	-0.3487	-0.1906	0.0367
Microdesmus lanceolatus	**-0.4152**	0.1520	0.1602
Micropogonias undulatus	0.3102	0.2026	-0.2157
Ophichthus spp.	-0.3290	0.3397	0.1944
Saurida brasiliensis	-0.1018	0.3291	**0.4753**
Scartella/Hypleurochilus (RA)	-0.0819	-0.3553	0.1492
Scomberomorus maculatus	0.0790	-0.2379	**0.3922**
Serranidae (RA)	0.1269	**0.4456**	0.2980
Sphyraena borealis	**-0.6769**	0.0186	0.1416
Symphurus spp.	0.0996	0.1954	**0.7694**

Environmental Variables	Correlations between environmental variables and their canonical variates		
	W1	W2	W3
Surface Salinity	**0.8923**	-0.0707	**-0.4225**
Surface Temperature	-0.1522	**-0.7550**	0.2641
Suspended Solids	0.2617	-0.1356	**0.6124**
Microzooplankton Biomass	**0.4352**	**0.5929**	**0.6644**

Table 21. Results of the canonical correlation analysis on log-transformed light trap CPUEs (15 most abundant taxa, and reef fish families) and environmental variables for VK 203. Loadings in bold under statistically significant canonical variables V1 and V2 explain at least 15% of the variation for that taxon. Loadings in bold under the environmental canonical variates W1 and W2 indicate the most influential environmental variables. RA = reef associated taxa, RD = reef dependent taxa.

Canonical Correlation	Likelihood Ratio	Approximate F	Pr > F
1) 0.773259	0.19717552	2.6970	0.0001
2) 0.518727	0.49039947	1.5354	0.0161

Taxa	Correlations between light trap CPUEs and their canonical variates	
	V1	V2
Auxis spp.	**0.6754**	-0.1477
Bregmaceros cantori	0.0468	0.3345
Caranx crysos	**0.5244**	-0.2060
Decapterus punctatus	-0.2085	0.0656
Eucinostomus spp.	-0.1354	0.0685
Euthynnus alletteratus	**0.5372**	-0.1012
Gobiidae	-0.0533	-0.0639
Hypsoblennius hentz/ionthas (RA)	0.3618	-0.1968
Hypsoblennius invemar (RA)	**-0.4034**	**-0.5151**
Lutjanidae (RA)	0.2125	**-0.4366**
Parablennius marmoreus (RA)	0.3097	0.1019
Pomacentrus spp. (RD)	**-0.6707**	**-0.4938**
Saurida brasiliensis	0.3361	-0.1655
Scartella/Hypleurochilus (RA)	0.0976	0.1729
Scomberomorus maculatus	0.0114	**0.5530**
Serranidae (RA)	-0.0705	0.1852
Synodus foetens	0.2703	0.0248

Environmental Variables	Correlations between environmental variables and their canonical variates	
	W1	W2
Surface Salinity	**0.9937**	-0.0675
Surface Temperature	-0.3390	-0.3715
Suspended Solids	0.1844	0.2321
Microzooplankton Biomass	0.1147	**0.9700**

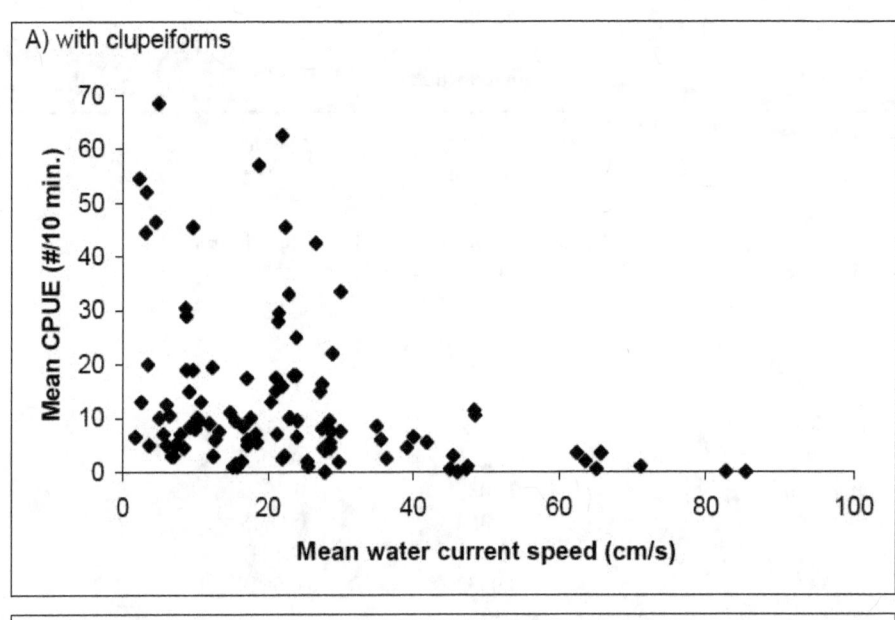

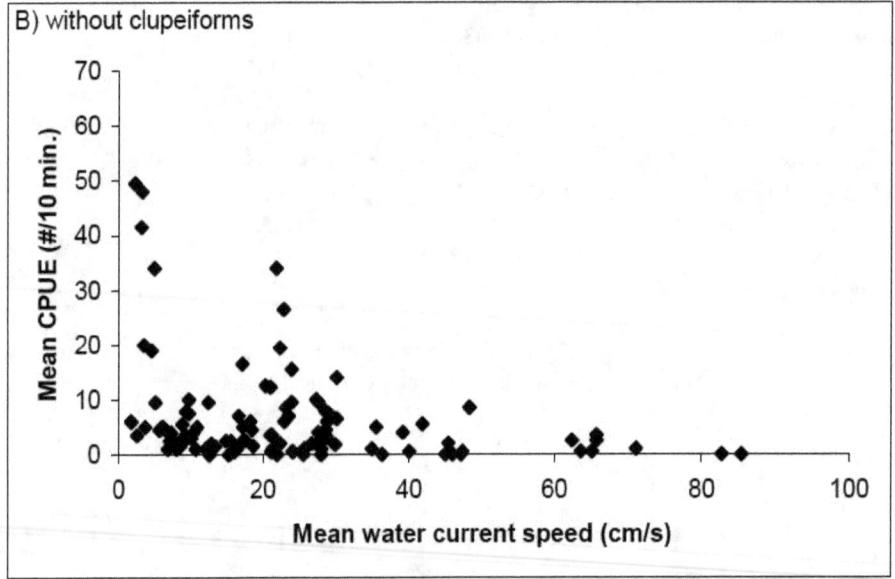

Figure 30. Scatter plots of water current speed versus mean CPUE from light traps at MP 259 and VK 203 combined, for data a) with clupeiforms and b) without clupeiforms included.

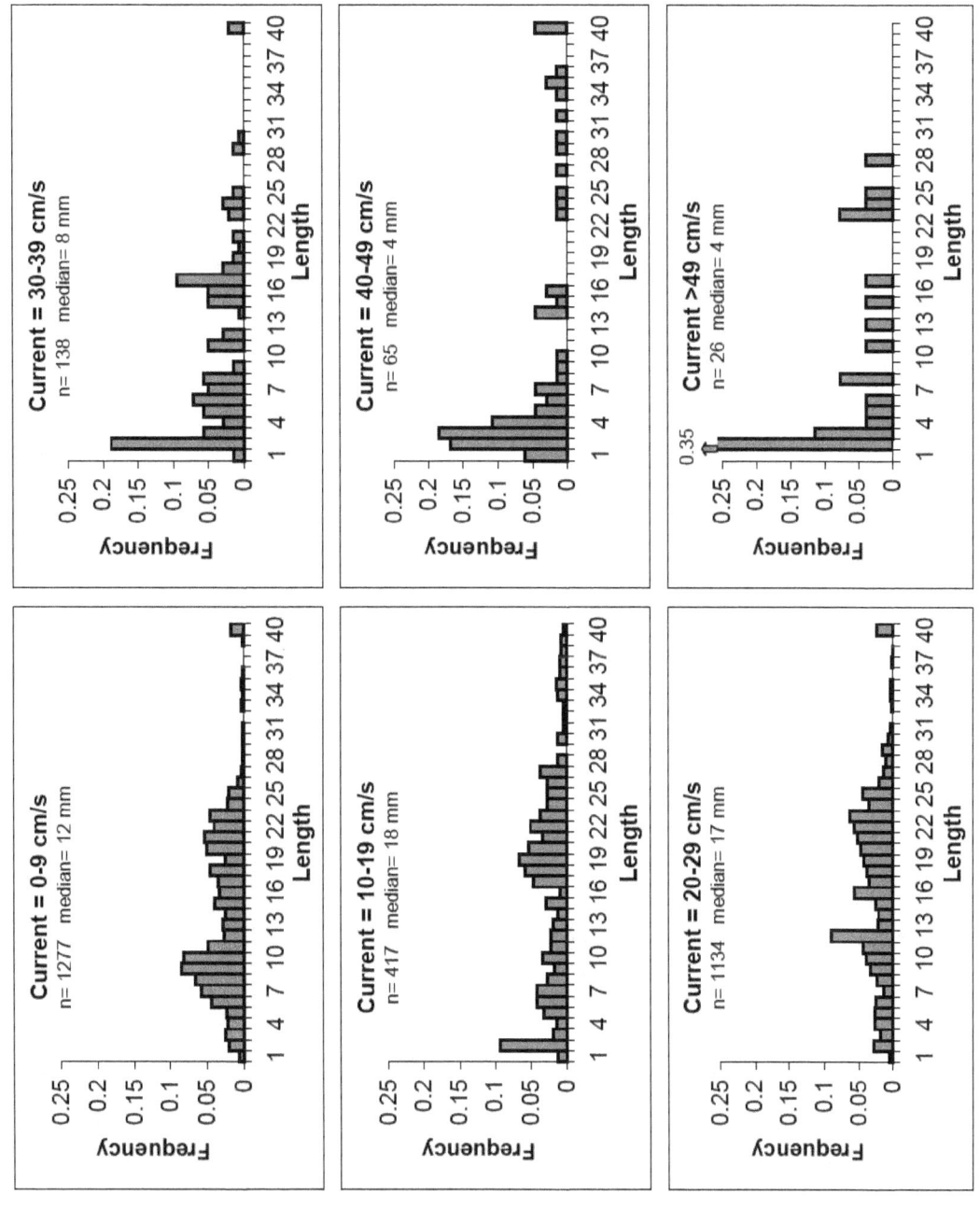

Figure 31. Size distributions of fishes, with clupeiforms included, collected in light traps from MP 259 and VK 203 combined at different water current speeds. Number of samples (n) and median lengths are included. Arrow above the bar points to the frequency for that length.

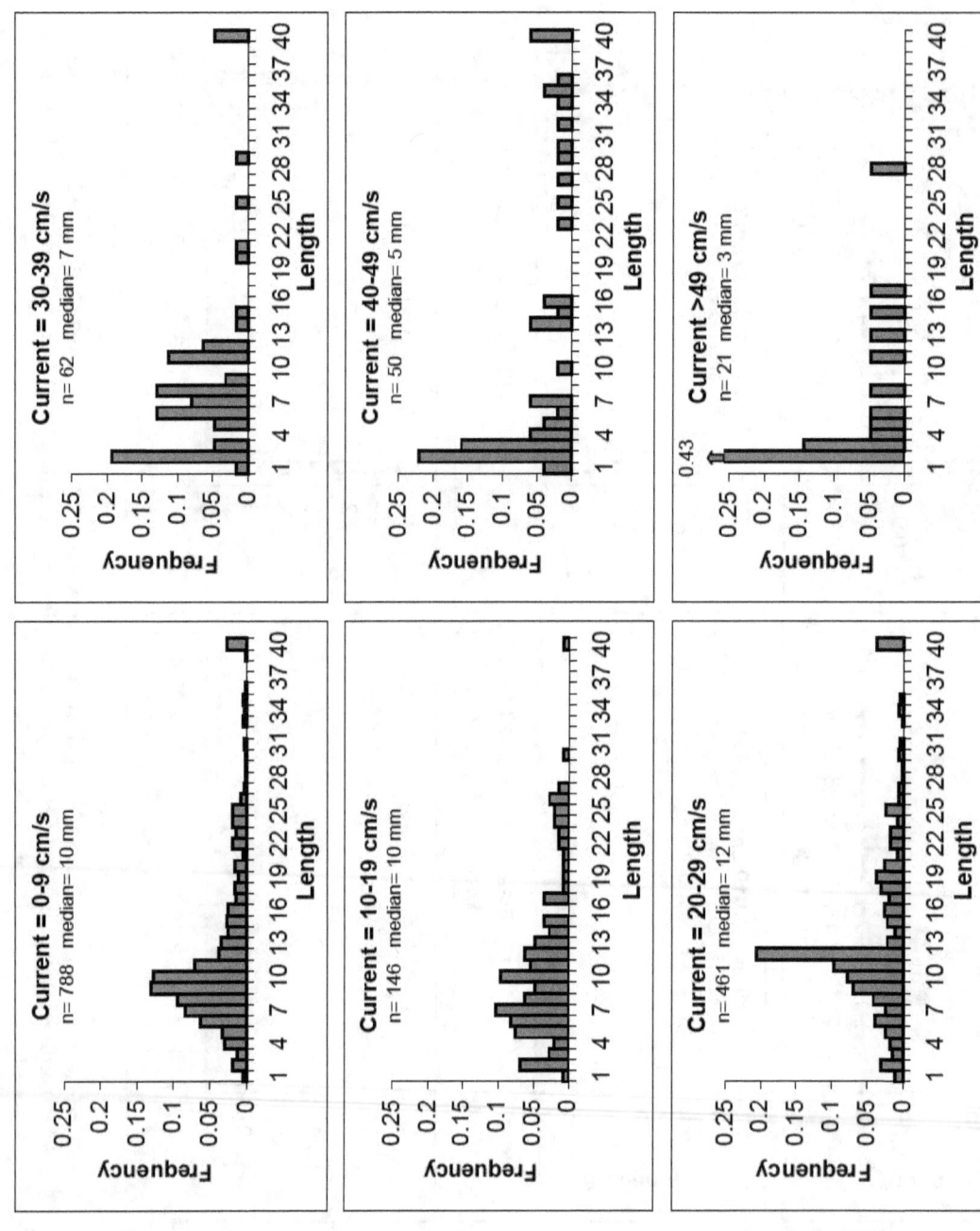

Figure 32. Size distributions of fishes, without clupeiforms included, collected in light traps, from MP 259 and VK 203 combined, at different water current speeds. Number of samples (n) and median lengths are included. Arrow above the bar points to the frequency for that length.

86

Size distributions of fishes, with and without clupeiforms included, collected by light traps at MP 259 and VK 203 combined were significantly different ($p < 0.05$) between all current speed intervals, except the two highest (i.e., 40-49 vs. >49 cm s^{-1}; Figures 31 and 32). At the highest current speeds the median lengths of fishes collected were below 5 mm, while at current speeds <30 cm s^{-1} the median lengths were 12-17 mm, with clupeiforms included, and 10-12 mm, without clupeiforms, and a wide range of sizes were collected.

Discussion

Across- and Along-Shelf Larval and Juvenile Fish Assemblages

Patterns of larval and juvenile fish abundance and diversity were primarily influenced by across-shelf gradients of increasing water depth. Densities of larval fishes from plankton nets were highest at the inner shelf platform ST 54 due mostly to high numbers of clupeiform larvae, which comprised 97% of the fish collected at this site (Figure 4a). However, when clupeiforms were removed densities remained highest at the shallowest platforms (Figure 4b). High numbers of ichthyoplankton are typical of coastal waters, as compared with offshore waters (Govoni et al. 1989; Grimes and Finucane 1991; Sabatés and Olivar 1996). Catch rates of larger postlarval and juvenile fishes showed a different pattern with highest catches at mid-shelf (Figure 5). Diversity and taxonomic richness also exhibited a peak at intermediate depths (Table 4). High diversity at intermediate depths may be the result of an overlap in the distributions of coastal and oceanic/tropical taxa, as observed for both adult demersal and platform fish assemblages (Sonnier et al. 1976; Gallaway 1981; Stanley and Wilson 2000). The inshore distribution of oceanic and tropical taxa may be limited by seasonal fluctuations in the nearshore environment, while the more oligotrophic conditions of the outer shelf may selectively remove coastal taxa that require higher prey concentrations.

The species composition of the non-clupeiform larval and juvenile fish assemblages collected at platforms also seemed to be structured by depth. Cluster analysis found three general assemblages: an inner shelf assemblage (ST 54), a mid-shelf assemblage (GI 94 and VK 203) and an outer shelf assemblage (GC 18 and MP 259; Figure 6). The inner shelf assemblage was dominated by *Cynoscion arenarius*, *Synodus foetens* and *Scomberomorus maculatus* (Table 5), and included high numbers of other typical coastal taxa, such as *Etropus crossotus*, *Menticirrhus* spp., *Peprilus burti* and *P. paru*. The mid-shelf assemblages were characterized by blenniids (particularly *Hypsoblennius invemar*), synodontids (particularly *Saurida brasiliensis*) and the bregmacerotid *Bregmaceros cantori* (Table 5). Unlike the other assemblages, which were dominated by demersal taxa, the outer shelf assemblages were primarily composed of pelagic (*Ariomma* spp., *Auxis* spp., *Caranx crysos*, and *Euthynnus alletteratus*) and mesopelagic taxa (*Cyclothone braueri* and Myctophidae; Tables 2 and 5).

These assemblages were similar to those found for across-shelf larval fish assemblages collected elsewhere (Houde et al. 1979; Sabatés and Olivar 1996; Thorrold and Williams 1996). In each of these studies there were strong differences between the larval fish assemblages inshore and those offshore. Several factors have been suggested to determine these large-scale distributions of larval fishes including: spawning behavior of adults, hydrographic conditions and differential mortality (Leis 1991). Because they generally agree with those found for adult populations (Houde 1981; Robins et al. 1986; Hoese and Moore 1998), the larval and juvenile fish distributions observed probably reflected the spawning behavior of adult fishes from nearby benthic, pelagic, and platform habitats. However, hydrographic conditions, such as the occasional offshore intrusion of low-salinity water, can alter larval fish assemblages by transporting coastal larvae to outer shelf regions (e.g., *Sciaenops ocellatus* and *C. arenarius* at GC 18; Hernandez et al. 2001).

Across-shelf changes in abundance were also observed for the reef fish larvae collected at platforms. On the inner shelf, blenniids (particularly *Scartella/Hypleurochilus* and *Hypsoblennius hentz/ionthas*) were the dominant reef taxa collected (Table 5). Other reef taxa were relatively rare (<10 individuals collected) and consisted of *Lutjanus campechanus*, *Rhomboplites aurorubens* and Serraninae. Reef taxa were most abundant at mid-shelf, and assemblages at these platforms included a high diversity of blenniids (*Hypsoblennius invemar*, *H. hentz/ionthas*, *Scartella/Hypleurochilus* and *Parablennius marmoreus*), lutjanids (*Lutjanus* spp., *L. campechanus*, and *R. aurorubens*), serranids (primarily *Diplectrum* spp., *Serranus* spp., and unidentified serranines) and pomacentrids (*Abudefduf* spp., *Chromis* spp. and *Pomacentrus* spp.). On the outer shelf, blenniids were not as abundant and reef taxa common at the shallower platforms were replaced by different taxa (i.e., *Pristipomoides aquilonaris* was the most abundant lutjanid, while anthiines and epinephelines were the most abundant serranids). Scarid, labrid and holocentrids larvae were also most common on the outer shelf. Higher abundance and diversity of larval and juvenile reef fishes at mid-shelf may be attributed to the high platform concentration in these areas (Tolan 2001). Because recruitment may be dependent on supply from nearby upstream reefs (Sale 1980; Doherty 1991), the proximity of the mid-shelf platforms to a greater number of potential sources (e.g., platforms) may favor a wider variety of taxa.

Similar transitions were observed in the adult reef fish assemblages at platforms in the northern Gulf. In the faunal assemblages described by Gallaway (1981), relatively low numbers of lutjanids and serranids characterized shallow platforms (<20 m), while a diverse assemblage of blenniids, lutjanids, pomacentrids and serranids were found at mid-depth (20-60 m) and chaetodontids, labrids, scarids, pomacentrids, and anthiine and epinepheline serranids were common at the outer shelf platforms (>60 m). From visual surveys at the platforms west of the Delta (GC 18, GI 94 and ST 54), lutjanids and serranids were most abundant and diverse at the mid-shelf platform, while reef taxa at the outer and inner shelf were dominated by *Paranthias furcifer*, and *Lutjanus campechanus* and *L. griseus*, respectively (Stanley and Wilson 2000).

The higher abundances of specific larvae in collections east or west of the Delta may be attributed to the proximity of the platforms to different habitats in the northeastern and northwestern Gulf. Larvae more abundant east of the Delta included: *Decapterus punctatus*, *Eucinostomus* spp., *Lutjanus* spp., *Microdesmus lanceolatus*, Ophichthidae, and *Thunnus* spp. Adults of several of these taxa are associated with habitats that are more common east of the Delta. For example, *Eucinostomus* spp. and certain species of Ophichthidae are among the dominant fishes in the pink shrimp-ground fish assemblage, which is associated with calcareous sediments of the northeastern Gulf (Chittenden and McEachern 1976, Robins et al. 1986). Furthermore, juvenile lutjanids (particularly *Lutjanus griseus* and *L. synagris*) are common in seagrass beds and mangroves, habitats that are also more common in the eastern Gulf (Patillo et al. 1997). Larvae more abundant west of the Delta included: *Caranx hippos/latus, Cynoscion arenarius, Euthynnus alletteratus, Peprilus burti, Scomberomorus cavalla,* and *Symphurus* spp. (Table 6). Populations of many of these species, particularly highly predaceous and fast growing taxa such as *C. hippos/latus, E. alletteratus* and *S. cavalla,* may be enhanced by the greater biological productivity associated with the Mississippi River discharge, which predominantly is a westerly flow from the Delta (Grimes and Kingsford 1996; Grimes 2001). Furthermore, the more estuarine conditions and softer sediments west of the Delta may provide more suitable habitat for adult *C. arenarius* and *Symphurus* spp. (Parker 1960; Hoese and Moore 1998).

Despite the more favorable hydrographic conditions and the availability of more suitable habitat in the northeastern Gulf (Briggs 1958; Smith 1976), differences in the abundance of reef-dependent larvae (e.g., pomacentrids, labrids and scarids) were not observed in collections east or west of the Delta. Juvenile and adult reef fish assemblages observed at platforms west of the Delta have been found to be more similar to shallow-water natural reef communities, which are more predominant in the northeastern Gulf, than they were to geographically-closer deep-water natural reef communities (Tolan 2001). Platforms, therefore, may facilitate the range-extension of shallow water reef taxa by providing shallow-water, hard substrate regardless of the water depth or location on the continental shelf (Dennis and Bright 1988; Tolan 2001).

Within- and Off-Platform Distribution of Larval and Juvenile Fishes

Greater numbers and higher diversity of postlarval and juvenile fishes were collected within the platform structure than in open waters up to 20 m away from the platform (Figure 7; Table 7). Similar results were found when within-platform light trap catches were compared to 20-m and 50-m off-platform light trap catches at VK 203, after the dominant *Hypsoblennius invemar* was removed from the data set. Studies on adult fish distributions have shown that platforms attracted greater densities and diversities than that typically found in open waters (Rooker et al. 1997; Stanley and Wilson 2000). Furthermore, this "platform-effect" decreased rapidly with distance from the platform (within 18-50 m; Stanley and Wilson 2000). Therefore, considering the relatively low CPUEs found off-platform, it is possible that the "platform-effect" for larval and juvenile fishes was within 20 m of the structure.

Clupeiforms (clupeids and engraulids) and synodontids were consistently collected in higher abundance within the platform than off-platform (Table 9). Though usually more abundant in pelagic habitats, clupeids and engraulids have been shown to be particularly photopositive (Choat et al. 1993; Brogan 1994) and would be strongly attracted to the platform's nighttime light field. Clupeiforms were collected in significantly greater abundance within-platform than off-platform, except at ST 54 and MP 259 (Table 8). The higher relative abundance of clupeiforms off-platform at ST 54 and MP 259 was probably responsible for the greater similarity between within- and off-platform light trap collections, and the higher diversities seen for off-platform light traps at these platforms (Table 7). Despite being significantly different in several instances, the size distributions of engraulids between within- and off-platform were generally very similar (Figure 8). The size distributions of synodontids also overlapped considerably, however, greater frequencies of larger individuals (>30 mm) were collected off-platform (Figure 9). Synodontids are pelagic until they metamorphose and settle to sand and mud bottoms at 30 to 45 mm in length (Jones et al. 1978; Leis and Rennis 2000a).

Therefore, it is probable that the individuals >30 mm collected off-platform represent individuals that are settling to benthic habitats adjacent to platforms.

Taxa collected primarily in waters down-current from the platform included scombrids and possibly carangids. Scombrids, particularly *Euthynnus alletteratus*, *Scomberomorus cavalla* and *S. maculatus*, were generally more abundant off-platform at each platform sampled (Table 9). The scombrids collected off-platform also occurred at larger sizes than within-platform (Figure 10). While the size distributions of *E. alletteratus* broadly overlapped, more individuals between 8 and 13 mm were found within-platform. Carangids were more evenly distributed between within- and off-platform, although *Caranx hippos/latus* was significantly more abundant off-platform at ST 54 and GC 18 (Table 9). Adult scombrids and carangids are large, predatory fishes that are commonly associated with the open waters around reefs, platforms or other structure, primarily because of the greater feeding opportunities at these locations (Gallaway 1981; Grimes et al. 1990; Choat and Bellwood 1991). The results from this study suggested that the open waters adjacent to platforms were the main habitat for postlarvae and juveniles. As larvae and juveniles, scombrids and carangids are highly predaceous and fast growing, and prey availability may be a critical factor for their early growth and survival (DeVries et al. 1990; Finucane et al. 1990; Lang et al. 1994). Therefore, scombrids and carangids may be utilizing concentrations of zooplankton and ichthyoplankton that may be attracted to the light field of platforms (Keenan et al. in press).

Reef fish, in general, did not show a consistent pattern of higher abundance within- or off-platform. Several blenniids (i.e., *Hypsoblennius hentz/ionthas* and *Scartella/Hypleurochilus*) were collected in higher numbers within-platform (Table 9). *Hypsoblennius invemar*, however, was more abundant off-platform at each platform except GI 94. Furthermore, this species was the dominant species collected in light traps deployed 50 m off-platform at VK 203 (Table 10). The size distributions of *H. invemar* were also significantly different between within- and off-platform (Figure 11). In each instance, fish collected off-platform were between 11 and 13 mm in length, while the lengths within-platform were generally smaller. *Pomacentrus* spp. were also found in higher abundances off-platform, but there was no difference in their size distributions (Table 9). The *H. invemar* and *Pomacentrus* spp. collected off-platform may represent settling fish as their sizes correspond to the sizes at settlement found for congeners (Robertson et al. 1988; Watson 1996a, 1996b, 2000). Once settled at platforms, these taxa would become more less available to light traps (Doherty 1991). Other reef taxa did not show consistent differences in their abundances between within- and off-platform. Lutjanids and serranids were significantly more abundant within-platform at GI 94, however, they were often more abundant off-platform (e.g., lutjanids at VK 203; Tables 9). The lack of consistent differences among platforms could be attributed to the grouping of individuals to the family level, however, separate analyses at lower taxonomic levels failed to show any clear patterns.

The few differences observed between the open water "background" (SEAMAP) and platform abundances of reef larvae were confounded by the large disparity in sampling effort between SEAMAP and platform surveys. In general, greater abundances of blenniids, holocentrids and pomacentrids were collected in platform plankton nets and light traps than in SEAMAP bongo tows and neuston nets (Tables 11-14). In contrast, serranids and labrids, and to some extent lutjanids, were generally more abundant in SEAMAP samples. The latter differences may be attributed to the larger volumes of water filtered per SEAMAP sample, which would increase the probability of encountering patches of reef fish larvae. For example, the mean volume of water filtered by plankton nets at GC 18 was 39.2 m^3 ($\pm$ 30.1, SD), while bongo nets at nearby SEAMAP stations filtered 259.2 m^3. Although estimates were unavailable, actively-towed neuston nets also probably sampled a greater volume of water than light traps. However, the larger number of samples taken at a platform may have counteracted the greater mean volume of water sampled at SEAMAP stations (e.g., 161 plankton net samples at GI 94 vs. 8 bongo net tows at SEAMAP stations; Table 11).

SEAMAP and platform samples were similar in that reef larvae, and especially reef-dependent larvae, were relatively rare. This rarity has been attributed to high mortality during the pelagic larval phase (near 100%; Leis 1991). Some researchers, however, have found that certain reef taxa, such as scarids, labrids, and acanthurids, occurred in greatest abundance in offshore waters up to 100 km from their natal reefs (Leis and Miller 1976; Victor 1987; Boehlert and Mundy 1993). While this may help explain the rarity of reef taxa at platform locations, it doesn't explain their low relative abundance in ichthyoplankton surveys in the open waters of the eastern Gulf and Caribbean (Richards 1984; Richards et al. 1993; Limouzy-Paris et al. 1994).

Lengths of larval reef fish collected by SEAMAP bongo nets were slightly smaller than those collected by platform plankton nets. Size distributions of serranids collected by bongo nets had a median length of 2 mm, while serranids collected by plankton nets had a median length of 3 mm (Figure 14). Similarly, the median length of lutjanids collected by bongo nets was 2 mm, compared to 4 mm for plankton net-collected lutjanids (Figure 15). These observed differences may be attributed to differences in the gears utilized to collect these larvae. Larvae were collected during SEAMAP surveys in a 333 μm mesh bongo net towed obliquely through the water column from near bottom (or to 200 m at the deeper stations) to the surface. Because the bongo nets were actively towed, larger larvae may have been able to avoid the net because of the pressure wave created (Choat et al. 1993). In contrast, the passively-fished, 333 μm mesh plankton net used at platforms may have encountered fewer avoidance problems.

Seasonal Patterns of Larval and Juvenile Fish Abundance at Platforms

The seasonality observed in larval and juvenile fish catches at the mid-shelf (VK 203) and outer-shelf (MP 259) platforms was similar to that observed from other studies in the northern Gulf. Peak plankton net densities and light trap CPUEs occurred during June-August at both platforms (Figures 16-19). Much of these higher catches were due to large abundances of clupeiforms, which have peak spawning during the spring and summer months (Finucane et al. 1979b; Houde et al. 1979; Ditty et al. 1988). High non-clupeiform catches during these months, at both VK 203 and MP 259, were attributed to other late spring and summer spawners such as *Auxis* spp., *Caranx crysos* and *Euthynnus alletteratus* (Ditty et al. 1988). A similar trend was observed during year-round sampling conducted at the outer shelf platform GC 18, although a secondary peak occurred during November due to high numbers of the fall-winter spawning *Mugil cephalus* (Hernandez 2001). High ichthyoplankton densities were also observed during the fall at VK 203 due to high numbers of the fall-winter spawning *Micropogonias undulatus* (Figure 18). *Sciaenops ocellatus* and *Peprilus burti* were also collected only during October at VK 203 (Table 3).

Most of the reef larvae collected at MP 259 and VK 203 were also generally found during the months of June-August (Tables 2 and 3). This was also the case during year-round sampling at GC 18 (Hernandez 2001), quarterly sampling at platforms in the northern Gulf (Tolan 2001), and other studies from the eastern and western Gulf (Finucane et al. 1979b; Houde et al. 1979; Ditty et al. 1988). However, anthiines were most abundant during September at MP 259, while serranines were most abundant during May at VK 203. These results were consistent with the seasonality reported for Anthinae and Serraninae larvae from other surveys of the Gulf (i.e., Anthinae in fall, Serraninae in spring; Houde 1982; McGowan 1985).

Lunar Periodicity

There was little difference in the total plankton net or light trap catches between full and new moons at MP 259 and VK 203, except for the total plankton net densities at VK 203, which were significantly higher on full moons (Figure 20). Without clupeiforms, new and full moon plankton net densities and light trap CPUEs were relatively similar to each other at both platforms. Other studies involving light-aggregation devices have found lower catches on full moons than on new moons, presumably due to the competitive interaction of lunar vs. lighted gear illumination (Gregory and Powles 1985; Rooker et al. 1996). It is possible that the platform's nighttime light field may have overridden any lunar effect that may have otherwise been present. Furthermore, differences in the total catch by lunar phase do not take into account the lunar-related behavior of individual taxa.

In a closer examination of reef taxa collected at platforms, there were strong differences in the numbers and developmental stages collected between new and full moons. Preflexion holocentrids and labrids were almost exclusively collected on full moons (Table 15). Preflexion *Hypsoblennius hentz/ionthas* and unidentified blenniids were found in significantly higher numbers on new moons, although these taxonomic groupings probably include many, if not all, of the species of blenniids collected at platforms. In contrast, preflexion *H. invemar*, *Scartella/Hypleurochilus* and many lutjanids, pomacentrids and serranids were collected in higher frequencies on new moons. Of the postflexion larvae, most blenniids, holocentrids, lutjanids, and pomacentrids were found in significantly higher numbers on new moons. *Lutjanus campechanus* were the only postflexion larvae found in higher numbers during full moons. The predominance of postflexion larvae collected on new moons was not surprising, because most were collected at, or near, settlement size; and numerous studies have documented higher rates of settlement during new moons (Victor 1986; Sponaugle and Cowen 1994; Rooker et al. 1996). Blenniids and pomacentrids, in particular, have settlement cycles that are associated with the darker periods of the lunar month, presumably to avoid visual predation (Robertson et al. 1988). Many reef taxa also exhibit lunar spawning cycles, which are often synchronized to maximize the amount of potential settlers available during the most favorable lunar phases (Robertson 1991). The relative lack of significant differences between lunar phases for preflexion larvae, as compared with postflexion larvae, was probably related to the effects of dispersal obscuring evidence of lunar spawning cycles (Doherty and Williams 1988; Meekan et al. 1993).

Temporal Variability of Plankton Net and Light Trap Catches

Coefficients of variation (CVs), calculated from the mean plankton net and light trap catches per sampling night and sampling trip, described pulses (or discrete peaks) in the catches of several dominant taxa and reef families at GI 94 and VK 203. Coefficients of variations among sampling nights were generally higher than, or approximately equal to, the CVs among sampling trips for nearly every taxa, indicating that mean catches on a nightly time-scale were more variable than mean catches by trip (Tables 16 and 17). However, the relative magnitude of both among night and among trip CVs was more informative in describing taxa with pulses. For example, plankton net-collected *Bregmaceros cantori* had CVs among the lowest at GI 94 and did not exhibit a discrete pulse (Figure 21). In contrast, light trap-collected *Hypsoblennius invemar* had CVs among the highest at both GI 94 and VK 203 and exhibited a large pulse, or two pulses at VK 203, in their nightly catch (Figures 21 and 22). This was also the case for light trap-collected Pomacentridae at both GI 94 and VK 203, even though among trip CVs were higher than among night CVs for this taxa at VK 203.

The pulses observed for *Hypsoblennius invemar* and Pomacentridae at both GI 94 and VK 203 probably represented settlement pulses. Most *H. invemar* and Pomacentridae collected during these pulses, at both platforms, were between 10-13 mm and 8-11 mm respectively, corresponding to the sizes at settlement reported for congeners (Robertson et al. 1988; Watson 1996a, 1996b, 2000). The occurrence of these pulses during darker periods of the lunar month (i.e., first quarter moon at GI 94 and new moons at VK 203) further suggests that they were settlement-related. Several studies have shown that reef fish year-classes were formed from settlement pulses lasting 1-3 nights (Robertson et al. 1988; Doherty 1991). One settlement pulse was found to contribute >40% of the year-class of a pomacentrid on the Great Barrier Reef (Pitcher 1988). While it is highly probable that the pulses observed at platforms represent settling fish, it is unknown how much, if at all, these pulses contribute to resident populations.

Another feature of these pulses was that they often coincided for different species and even different families. This was particularly noticeable for *Hypsoblennius invemar* and Pomacentridae, which simultaneously exhibited pulses in light trap samples at both GI 94 and VK 203 (Figures 21 and 22). A similar pulse at MP 259 comprised most of the holocentrids, pomacentrids, synodontids, and *H. invemar* collected at this platform. Multitaxa pulses have also been documented during other studies. For example, a recruitment pulse observed on the Great Barrier Reef was composed of three species of pomacentrids (Williams 1983). Also near the Great Barrier Reef, most pomacentrids, lethrinids and mullids collected by light traps during a survey were taken at the same station during the same 3-night period (Thorrold and Williams 1996). Such pulses have been attributed to the lunar entrainment of settlement cycles (Doherty 1991). However, the synodontids, holocentrids and *H. invemar* collected during the multitaxa pulse at MP 259 were not at settlement size. It is possible that these taxa were entrained within a common water mass that led to a presettlement aggregation of larvae composed of several species (Sweatman 1988; Kingsford and Choat 1989).

Much of the within-night variability in total plankton net and light trap catches could be attributed to variability in catches of clupeiforms. Mean densities and CPUEs by hour after sunset were extremely variable with peaks occurring throughout the night at any specific platform (Figure 23). Without clupeiforms, densities and CPUEs were surprisingly equal throughout the night, except at VK 203 and GC 18 where clupeiforms were not as abundant (Figure 24; Table 8). There was no obvious evidence of nocturnal vertical migration by larval fish. Many taxa of larval fish undertake vertical migrations up into the neuston at dusk, followed by a return to depth at dawn (Kendall and Naplin 1981; Leis 1986, 1991). Such movements may have been missed during this study due to the absence of samples at either dusk or dawn. Furthermore, analyses of the total ichthyoplankton catches (with or without clupeiforms) may have masked the behavior of individual taxa. Separate analyses of the within-night catches of dominant taxa and reef taxa, however, were also inconclusive, with high degrees of variability throughout the night across the different platforms.

Length-Frequency and Developmental Stages of Reef Taxa

One of the proposed fisheries benefits of platforms is that they may provide new spawning habitat. Although not directly observed, recent and nearby spawning by reef fish was inferred by the collection of recently-hatched or very small larvae at platforms. Many recently-hatched and preflexion blenniid, lutjanid and serranid larvae were collected at every platform, indicating local spawning events (Figures 24-26). In addition, relatively small preflexion holocentrids and pomacentrids were collected at the mid-shelf platform GI 94, and preflexion holocentrids, labrids and scarids were collected at the outer shelf platforms, MP 259 and GC 18 (Figures 27-29). Although the presence of these young larvae is indicative of local spawning, it is not known whether this spawning occurred at platforms or nearby natural reefs. Seasonal transport envelopes, created from satellite altimetry data and otolith-derived pelagic transport durations, have been created for serranid larvae collected at three mid- and outer shelf platforms (Tolan 2001). Within these envelopes, other oil and gas platforms were numerically dominant over natural reefs, statistically making platforms the most probable source of the larvae.

Another proposed fishery benefit of platforms is that they may provide new nursery/settlement habitat or refugia. Again using the length frequency of reef fish collected at platforms, the presence of settlement-size larvae could provide indirect evidence for a potential nursery habitat function. Of the potential settlers, blenniids were the most abundant settlement-size reef larvae, and pomacentrids were the most common settlement-size reef-dependent larvae collected at platforms (Figures 24 and 28). Considering that blenniids and pomacentrids were often collected in discrete pulses during the darker lunar phases (new and first quarter; Figures 21 and 22), as reported for other settling fish from these families, it is highly likely that these taxa were settling on platforms. Furthermore, efforts to collect new settlers in settlement traps were attempted at MP 259 and VK 203 (unpublished data). Although catches were low, blenniids and pomacentrids were the most common taxa and were collected at size ranges beginning where sizes from light traps ended (i.e., ≥14 mm).

Settlement-size larvae of other reef taxa were relatively rare, as compared with blenniids and pomacentrids, and were represented mostly by lutjanids at the mid-shelf platforms (Figure 25). The relatively low numbers of settlement-size lutjanids and serranids was not surprising because many of these taxa have been shown to settle out in alternative, more coastal nursery habitats, such as sea grass beds, mangroves, or low relief hard substrate (Lindeman 1989; Beets and Hixon 1994; Szedlmayer and Conti 1998). However, juvenile *Lutjanus* spp. have also been collected west of the Delta in association with rock jetties (Hernandez 2001). Although larger postflexion, rhynchichthys-stage holocentrids were collected at MP 259 and GC 18 (Figure 27), these individuals probably represented presettlement stages as holocentrids have extended larval durations (pelagic specimens up to 48 mm; Leis and Rennis 2000b)

The relative abundance of settlement-size reef larvae at platforms may be influenced by two disparate spawning strategies exhibited by reef fishes: broadcast spawning of pelagic eggs or benthic spawning of demersal adhesive eggs. The most abundant settlement-size larvae at platforms were from the benthic-spawning families Blenniidae and Pomacentridae. The other reef families of interest in this study were from pelagic-spawning families and were either absent (Acanthuridae and Pomacanthidae), rare (Chaetodontidae and Labridae) or predominantly collected in presettlement stages (Holocentridae, Lutjanidae, Scaridae and Serranidae). The differences in relative supply of potential settlers are probably related to early life history traits that are often associated with the two spawning strategies. In general, as compared to benthic eggs, pelagic eggs are smaller and result in less developmentally-advanced larvae that have longer larval durations and may, therefore, be more vulnerable to predation and advective loss (Cowen and Sponaugle 1997). Furthermore, the transition from pelagic to reef environments is often characterized by high levels of predation by resident fishes (the "wall of mouths", Hamner et al. 1988). Therefore, the probability of recruitment for pelagically-spawned larvae may be considerably low. Because they generally have shorter larval durations, benthically-spawned larvae probably have limited dispersal and may be able to remain in areas where suitable settlement habitat is more available (Barlow 1981). This may explain, in part, the high abundance of postflexion and settlement-size blenniids and pomacentrids at the mid-shelf platforms, which reside in areas of high platform concentration (Tolan 2001).

Environmental Variables and Larval and Juvenile Fish Abundances

Seasonal variations in temperature influenced the abundances of several taxa at the outer shelf platform MP 259. Plankton net-collected *Auxis* spp., *Euthynnus alletteratus* and *Symphurus* spp. were positively associated with temperature (Table 18), and represent taxa with peak larval abundance during the spring and summer months (Ditty et al. 1988). In contrast, plankton net-collected *Bregmaceros cantori*, Myctophidae and Serranidae were negatively associated with temperature, which is consistent with their peak larval abundances during the spring and fall in the northern Gulf (Houde 1982; McGowan 1985; Ditty et al. 1988).

Several taxa were associated with different water masses that occurred at MP 259. Two prominent features exhibited by plots of environmental variables at MP 259 were the relatively low salinity, high turbidity waters that occurred during late May and late August, and the relatively high salinity, low turbidity water during early July (Figure 2). *Scomberomorus maculatus* in plankton nets and *Chloroscombrus chrysurus* in light traps seemed to be associated with the lower salinity waters (Tables 18 and 19). Because larvae of *S. maculatus* and *C. chrysurus* have been found in highest densities in the shallower, coastal sections of the Gulf (Patillo et al. 1997; Hernandez 2001), these taxa were probably advected offshore by an intrusion of coastal water. In contrast, light trap-collected *Decapterus punctatus*, *Holocentrus* spp., *Hypsoblennius invemar*, *Pomacentrus* spp. and *Synodus foetens* were associated with the high salinity, low turbidity water mass (Table 19). The reasons for this association are not evident, however, as previously discussed, it is possible that some of these taxa (i.e., *H. invemar* and *Pomacentrus* spp.) may have been part of a settlement pulse. Considering that non-clupeiform light trap catches were 4 to 5 times greater during the early July sampling trip than other sampling trips (Figure 17), it is also possible that some oceanographic event may have entrained, concentrated and transported these postflexion and juvenile fishes to MP 259.

There was less environmental variability at the mid-shelf platform VK 203, and consequently microzooplankton biomass was the most influential environmental variable for larval and juvenile fish abundances. Taxa positively associated with this variable included *Bregmaceros cantori*, *Etropus crossotus*, *Saurida brasiliensis*, *Scomberomorus maculatus* and *Symphurus* spp. in plankton nets and *S. maculatus* in light traps (Tables 20 and 21). Serranidae were also positively associated with microzooplankton biomass, but were only collected when temperatures were relatively cooler (Table 20). These results are not surprising because zooplankton are a patchy resource and fish larvae that are associated with high prey densities often benefit from enhanced growth and survival (Hunter 1981; Grimes 2001). However, light trap-collected *Hypsoblennius invemar*, *Pomacentrus* spp. and Lutjanidae were negatively associated with microzooplankton biomass (Table 21). Similar to MP 259, these taxa may have been associated with settlement pulses that occurred coincidentally with low prey biomass.

Effects of Water Current Speed on Light Trap Catches

Light trap catch efficiency seemed to be affected by high current speeds at MP 259 and VK 203. At current speeds greater than 30 cm s^{-1} light trap CPUEs, with or without clupeiforms included, were <10 fish/10 min., while at lower current speeds catch rates were often above 20 fish/10 min. (Figure 30). Doherty (1987) speculated that for fixed light traps (light traps that are not allowed to drift freely with the current) catches should increase initially with faster currents as more water is sampled, but then decrease as current speed interferes with the catchability of larval fish. At this point, catchability would be highly dependent on the ability of a larval fish to swim to the light trap. While a dome-shaped relationship was not evident from the results of this study, a change in fish catchability was observed. At higher current speeds (>40 cm s^{-1}) the median length of fish collected by light traps, with or without clupeiforms, was less than 10 mm, while at lower current speeds median lengths were above 10 mm and a wide range of sizes were collected (Figure 31 and 32). The larvae <10 mm in length collected at the higher current speeds were undoubtedly passively entrained in the light trap gear. Larger postlarvae and juveniles were seemingly relatively unavailable to light traps at high current speeds. Swimming speeds of fish larvae, in general, have been measured at 1-5 body lengths sec^{-1} for sustained swimming and 10-20 body lengths sec^{-1} for burst-swimming speeds (Blaxter 1986). Therefore, for the average 20 mm fish burst-swimming speeds would be 20-40 cm s^{-1}. At these swimming speeds it would be difficult for a fish to maneuver to and enter a light trap at the highest current speeds observed.

Conclusions

This study represents an important step towards understanding the ecological significance of oil and gas platforms to the early life history stages of fishes. Given the extensive network of platforms in the northern Gulf, it is important to determine what species are associated with platforms and how they affect larval and juvenile fish assemblages, including whether they provide nursery/recruitment habitat for postlarval and juvenile fishes. Such information is necessary to determine whether platforms, and artificial reefs in general, contribute to the new production of fish.

The synthesis of data from platforms east of the Mississippi River Delta with data from platforms west of the Delta allowed us to characterize the larval and juvenile fish assemblages collected at platforms across longitudinal and latitudinal gradients. Similar to adult fish distributions (Hoese and Moore 1998; Stanley and Wilson 2000), the larval and juvenile fish assemblages seemed to be influenced by across-shelf gradients of increasing depth. High larval densities of coastal taxa such as sciaenids, synodontids and *Scomberomorus maculatus* characterized inner shelf non-clupeiform assemblages. Mid-shelf assemblages were comprised of a high diversity of larval and juvenile blenniids, synodontids, bregmacerotids and scombrids. Outer shelf catches were generally poor, and primarily composed of scombrids, carangids, and other oceanic taxa. Reef taxa were most abundant and diverse at the mid-shelf platforms, due to large numbers of larval and juvenile blenniids, pomacentrids and lutjanids. This high abundance and diversity at mid-shelf could be attributed to the high concentration of platforms (i.e., more potential sources of larvae) and the favorable environmental conditions at mid-shelf (Parker 1960; Gallaway 1981; Tolan 2001). The only differences observed in the larval and juvenile fish assemblages across longitudinal gradients (i.e., east or west of the Delta) were differences in the abundance of certain taxa. Higher abundance of these taxa east or west of the Delta may, in turn, reflect differences in the hydrographic conditions and/or habitat availability. Despite the higher concentration of natural reef-type habitats east of the Delta, reef larvae were not more abundant at platforms in these areas. The extensive network of platforms may have allowed for the range extension of reef taxa that would otherwise be limited by the availability of hard-substrate in the northern Gulf (Dennis and Bright 1988; Tolan 2001).

The higher abundance and diversity of postlarval and juvenile fishes within the platform structure, as compared with adjacent down-current open waters, indicates that platforms have a significant impact on the distribution of postlarval and juvenile fishes in the northern Gulf. Platforms represent structure in the pelagic habitat, and concentrations of larval and juvenile fishes have often been found associated with biotic or abiotic structure (Kingsford 1993). Light trap collections from within the platform were dominated by clupeids, engraulids and presettlement synodontids. These typically pelagic fishes may have been attracted by the nighttime light-fields of the platforms and/or concentrations of prey that may be found in the waters around platforms. Although generally more abundant away from the platform, highly predatory scombrids and carangids also may be opportunistically utilizing platform areas for increased feeding opportunities. Therefore, populations of clupeids, engraulids and scombrids, which would otherwise spend considerable time foraging for prey in the pelagic environment, may benefit from the presence of platforms, particularly in more oligotrophic offshore waters. However, increased prey availability may be offset by increased predation from the large populations of adult fishes at platforms.

Platforms may provide nursery/recruitment habitat for certain reef taxa. Blenniids and pomacentrids, the most common reef taxa collected at platforms, were predominantly collected as settlement-size individuals. These settlement-size fishes were most often collected in discrete pulses during the darker lunar phases (i.e., new and first quarter moons), which is typical of other settling reef fishes. The fact that blenniids and pomacentrids generally have short larval durations, and, therefore, limited dispersal and advective loss, further increases the probability that these taxa may use platforms as nursery/recruitment habitat. Other reef taxa collected at platforms (e.g., labrids, lutjanids and serranids) were rare or predominantly collected as presettlement larvae. The lack of settlement-size larvae from these taxa does not preclude the possibility that these taxa use platforms as nursery/recruitment habitat. It is possible that pulses of settling reef larvae could have been missed, or larvae may have settled to benthic habitats at the base of the platform, areas that were beyond the reach of the sampling gear utilized. During this study, the areas sampled at platforms represented shallow water hard-substrate, habitat that is obviously limited on the continental shelf of the northern Gulf. Because artificial reefs most likely benefit species that are habitat-limited (Bohnsack 1989), platforms should, therefore, enhance the production of typical shallow water reef taxa (e.g., blenniids and pomacentrids).

LITERATURE CITED

Barlow, G.W. 1981. Patterns of parental investment, dispersal and size among coral-reef fishes. Environmental Biology of Fishes 6: 65-85.

Bedinger, C.A., J.W. Cooper, A. Kwok, R.E. Childers, and K.T. Kimball. 1980. Ecological investigations of petroleum production platforms in the central Gulf of Mexico. Volume 1: Pollutant fate and effects studies. Draft final report submitted to the Bureau of Land Management, Contract AA551-CT8-17.

Beets, J. and M.A. Hixon. 1994. Distribution, persistence, and growth of groupers (Pisces: Serranidae) on artificial and natural patch reefs in the Virgin Islands. Bulletin of Marine Science 55: 470-483.

Blaxter, J.H.S. 1986. Development of sense organs and behaviour of teleost larvae with special reference to feeding and predator avoidance. Transactions of the American Fisheries Society 115: 98-114.

Boehlert, G.W. and B.C. Mundy. 1993. Ichthyoplankton assemblages at seamounts and oceanic islands. Bulletin of Marine Science 53: 336-361.

Bohnsack, J.A. 1989. Are high densities of fishes at artificial reefs the result of habitat limitations or behavioral preference? Bulletin of Marine Science 44: 632-645.

Bohnsack, J.A. 1991. Habitat structure and the design of artificial reefs. In: Bell, S.S., E.D. McCoy and H.R. Mushinsky, eds. Habitat Structure: The Physical Structure of Objects in Space. London: Chapman Hall.

Bohnsack, J.A. and D.L. Sutherland. 1985. Artificial reef research: a review with recommendations for future priorities. Bulletin of Marine Science 37:11-19.

Bohnsack, J.A., D.E. Harper, D.B. McClellan and M. Hulsbeck. 1994. Effects of reef size on colonization and assemblage structure of fishes at artificial reefs off southeastern Florida, U.S.A. Bulletin of Marine Science 55: 796-823.

Bortone, S.A. 1998. Resolving the attraction-production dilemma in artificial reef research: Some yeas and nays. Fisheries 23: 6-10.

Briggs, J.C. 1958. A list of Florida fishes and their distribution. Bulletin of the Florida State Museum Biological Sciences 2(8): 223-318.

Brogan, M.W. 1994. Two methods of sampling fish larvae over reefs: a comparison from the Gulf of California. Marine Biology 118: 33-44.

Chittenden, M.E. and J.D. McEachran. 1976. Composition, ecology, and dynamics of demersal fish communities on the northwestern Gulf of Mexico continental shelf, with a similar synopsis for the entire gulf. TAMU-SG-76-2008. College Station: Texas A&M University.

Choat, J.H. and D.R. Bellwood. 1991. Reef fishes: their history and evolution. In Sale, P.F., ed. The ecology of fishes on coral reefs. San Diego: Academic Press.

Choat, J.H, P.J. Doherty, B.A. Kerrigan, and J.M. Leis. 1993. A comparison of towed nets, purse seine, and light-aggregation devices for sampling larvae and pelagic juveniles of coral reef fishes. Fishery Bulletin 91: 195-209.

Continental Shelf Associates. 1982. Study of the effect of oil and gas activities on reef fish populations in the Gulf of Mexico OCS area. U.S. Department of the Interior, Minerals Management Service, Gulf of Mexico OCS Region, New Orleans, LA. MMS Contract No. AA551-CT-9-36.

Cowen, R.K. and S. Sponaugle. 1997. Relationships between early life history traits and recruitment among coral reef fishes. In: R.C. Chambers and E.A. Trippel, eds. Early life history and recruitment in fish populations. Chapman and Hall, New York.

Dennis, G.D. and T.J. Bright. 1988. Reef fish assemblages on hard banks in the northwestern Gulf of Mexico. Bulletin of Marine Science 43(2): 280-307.

DeVries, D.A., C.B. Grimes, K.C. Lang, and D.B. White. 1990. Age and growth of king and Spanish mackerel larvae and juveniles from the Gulf of Mexico and U.S. south Atlantic. Environmental Biology of Fishes 29: 135-143.

Ditty, J.G., G.G. Zieske, and R.F. Shaw. 1988. Seasonality and depth distribution of larval fishes in the northern Gulf of Mexico above latitude 26°00' N. Fishery Bulletin 86: 811-823.

Doherty, P.J. 1987. Light-traps: selective but useful devices for quantifying the distribution and abundances of larval fishes. Bulletin of Marine Science 41: 423-431.

Doherty, P.J. 1991. Spatial and temporal patterns in recruitment. In Sale, P.F., ed. The ecology of fishes on coral reefs. San Diego: Academic Press.

Doherty, P.J. and D. McB. Williams. 1988. The replenishment of coral reef fish populations. Oceanography and Marine Biology Annual Reviews 26: 487-551.

Finucane, J.H., L.A. Collins, and L.E. Barger. 1979a. Determine the effects of discharges on seasonal abundance, distribution, and composition of ichthyoplankton in the oil field. In: Jackson, W.B., ed. Environmental Assessment of an active oil field in the Northwestern Gulf of Mexico, 1977-1978. NOAA Report to EPA, Contract Number EPA-IAG-D%-E693-EO, NMFS Southeast Fisheries Center, Galveston.

Finucane, J.H., L.A. Collins, L.E. Barger, and J.D. McEachran. 1979b. Ichthyoplankton/mackerel eggs and larvae. In: Jackson, W.B., ed. Environmental Studies of the South Texas Outer Continental Shelf 1976. Contract Number AA550-TA7-3. NOAA Final Report to BLM, NMFS Southeast Fisheries Center, Galveston.

Finucane, J.H., C.B. Grimes, and S.P. Naughton. 1990. Diets of young king and Spanish mackerel off the southeast United States. Northeast Gulf Science 11: 145-153.

Gallaway, B.J. 1981. An ecosystem analysis of oil and gas development on the Texas-Louisiana continental shelf. FWS/OBS-81/27. U.S. Fish & Wildlife Service, Office of Biological Services, Washington, D.C.

Gallaway, B.J. 1999. Delineation of essential habitat for juvenile red snapper in the northwestern Gulf of Mexico. Transactions of the American Fisheries Society. 128: 713-726.

Gallaway, B.J. and L.R. Martin. 1980. Volume III-Effects of gas and oil field structures and effluents on pelagic and reef fishes, demersal fishes and macrocrustaceans. In Jackson, W.B. and E.P. Wilkens, eds. Environmental assessment of Buccaneer Gas and Oil Field in the northwestern Gulf of Mexico, 1978-1979. NOAA Technical Memorandum, NMFS-SEFC-37.

Govoni, J.J., D.E. Hoss, and D.R. Colby. 1989. The spatial distribution of larval fishes about the Mississippi River plume. Limnology and Oceanography. 34: 178-187.

Gregory, R.S. and P.M. Powles. 1985. Chronology, distribution, and sizes of larval fish sampled by light traps in macrophytic Chemung lake. Canadian Journal of Zoology 63: 2569-2577.

Grimes, C.B. 2001. Fishery production and the Mississippi River discharge. Fisheries 26: 17-26.

Grimes, C. B. and J.H. Finucane. 1991. Spatial distribution and abundance of larval and juvenile fish, chlorophyll and macrozooplankton around the Mississippi River discharge plume, and the role of the plume in fish recruitment. Marine Ecology Progress Series. 75: 109-119.

Grimes, C.B. and M.J. Kingsford. 1996. How do riverine plumes of different sizes influence fish larvae: do they enhance recruitment? Marine and Freshwater Research 47: 191-208.

Grimes, C.B., J.H. Finucane, L.A. Collins, and D.A. DeVries. 1990. Young king mackerel in the Gulf of Mexico, a summary of the distribution and occurrence of larvae and juveniles, and spawning dates for Mexican juveniles. Bulletin of Marine Science 46(3): 640-654.

Hamner, W.M., M.S. Jones, J.H. Carleton, J.R. Hauri and D. McB. Williams. 1988. Zooplankton, planktivorous fish, and water currents on a windward reef face: Great Barrier Reef, Australia. Bulletin of Marine Science 42: 459-479.

Hastings, R.W. 1976. Observations on the fish fauna associated with offshore platforms in the northeastern Gulf of Mexico. Fishery Bulletin 74: 387-402.

Hernandez, F.J., Jr. 2001. The across-shelf distribution of larval, postlarval and juvenile fishes collected at oil and gas platforms and a coastal jetty off Louisiana west of the Mississippi River Delta. Ph.D. Dissertation. Louisiana State University, Baton Rouge.

Hernandez, F.J., Jr., R.F. Shaw, J.C. Cope, J.G. Ditty, M.C. Benfield and T. Farooqi. 2001. Across-shelf larval, postlarval, and juvenile fish communities collected at offshore oil and gas platforms and a coastal rock jetty west of the Mississippi River Delta. Prepared by the Coastal Fisheries Institute, Louisiana State University, U.S. Department of the Interior, Minerals Management Service, Gulf of Mexico OCS Region, New Orleans, LA. OCS Study MMS 2001-077. 144pp.

Hernandez, F.J., Jr., R.F. Shaw, J.S. Cope, J.G. Ditty, T. Farooqi and M.C. Benfield. In Press. The across-shelf larval, postlarval, and juvenile fish assemblages collected at offshore oil and gas platforms west of the Mississippi River Delta. American Fisheries Society Special Symposium Series.

Hildebrand, H.H. 1954. A study of the fauna of the brown shrimp (*Penaeus aztecus* Ives) grounds in the western Gulf of Mexico. Publications of the Institute of Marine Science. 3: 233-366.

Hixon, M.A. and J.P. Beets. 1989. Shelter characteristics and Caribbean fish assemblages: experiments with artificial reefs. Bulletin of Marine Science 44: 666-680.

Hoese, H.D. and R.H. Moore. 1998. Fishes of the Gulf of Mexico: Texas, Louisiana, and Adjacent Waters. College Station: Texas A&M University Press. 422 pp.

Houde, E.D. 1981. Distribution and abundance of four types of codlet (Pisces: Bregmacerotidae) larvae from the eastern Gulf of Mexico. Biological Oceanography 1: 81-104.

Houde, E.D. 1982. Kinds, distributions and abundances of sea bass larvae (Pisces: Serranidae) from the eastern Gulf of Mexico. Bulletin of Marine Science 32(2): 511-522.

Houde, E.D., J.C. Leak, C.E. Dowd, S.A. Berkeley, and W.J. Richards. 1979. Ichthyoplankton abundance and diversity in the eastern Gulf of Mexico. Report to the Bureau of Land Management. Contract AA550-CT7-28. NTIS PB-299839.

Hunter, J.R. 1981. Feeding ecology and predation of marine fish larvae. In: R. Lasker, ed. Marine Fish Larvae: Morphology, Ecology and Relation to Fisheries. University of Washington Press, Seattle, Washington.

Johannes, R.E. 1978. Reproductive strategies of coastal marine fishes in the tropics. Environmental Biology of Fishes 3: 65-84.

Jones, P.W., F.D. Martin, and J.D. Hardy, Jr. 1978. Development of fishes of the Mid-Atlantic Bight: an atlas of egg, larval and juvenile stages. Volume 1: Acipenseridae through Ictaluridae. Center for Environmental and Estuarine Studies of the University of Maryland. Prepared for U.S. Fish and Wildlife Service. Biological Services Program. FWS/OBS-78/12. 366 pp.

Keenan, S.F., M.C. Benfield, and R.F. Shaw. In Press. Zooplanktivory by blue runner *Caranx crysos*: a potential energetic subsidy to Gulf of Mexico fish populations at petroleum platforms. American Fisheries Society Special Symposium Series.

Kendall, A.W., Jr. and N.A. Naplin. 1981. Diel-depth distribution of summer ichthyoplankton in the Middle Atlantic Bight. Fishery Bulletin 79(4): 705-726.

Kingsford, M.J. and J.H. Choat. 1989. Horizontal distribution patterns of presettlement reef fish: Are they influenced by the proximity of reefs. Marine Biology 101: 285-297.

Kingsford, M.J. 1993. Biotic and abiotic structure in the pelagic environment: importance to small fish. Bulletin of Marine Science 53: 393-415.

Krebs, C. J. 1999. Ecological Methodology, second edition. Addison-Wesley Educational Publishers Incorporated. Reading, Massachusetts.

Lang, K.L., C.B. Grimes, and R.F. Shaw. 1994. Variations in the age and growth of yellowfin tuna larvae, *Thunnus albacares*, collected about the Mississippi River plume. Environmental Biology of Fishes 39: 259-270.

Leis, J.M. 1986. Vertical and horizontal distribution of fish larvae near coral reefs at Lizard Island, Great Barrier Reef. Marine Biology. 90: 505-516.

Leis, J.M. 1991. Vertical distribution of fish larvae in the Great Barrier Reef Lagoon, Australia. Marine Biology 109: 157-166.

Leis, J.M. and J.M. Miller. 1976. Offshore distributional patterns of Hawaiian fish larvae. Marine Biology 36: 359-367.

Leis, J.M. and D.S. Rennis. 2000a. Synodontidae. In: J.M. Leis and B.M. Carson-Ewart, eds. The larvae of Indo-Pacific coastal fishes: an identification guide to marine fish larvae. Fauna Malesiana Handbooks. Boston, MA: Brill Publishing. 850 pp.

Leis, J.M. and D.S. Rennis. 2000b. Holocentridae. In: J.M. Leis and B.M. Carson-Ewart, eds. The larvae of Indo-Pacific coastal fishes: an identification guide to marine fish larvae. Fauna Malesiana Handbooks. Boston, MA: Brill Publishing. 850 pp.

Limouzy-Paris, C., M.F. McGowan, W.J. Richards, J.P. Umaran and S.S. Cha. 1994. Diversity of fish larvae in the Florida Keys: Results from SEFCAR. Bulletin of Marine Science 54(3): 857-870.

Lindeman, K.C. 1989. Coastal construction, larval settlement and early juvenile habitat use in grunts, snappers and other coastal fishes of southeast Florida. Bulletin of Marine Science 44: 1068.

Magurran, A.E. 1988. Ecological Diversity and Its Measurement. Princeton: Princeton University Press.

McGowan, M.F. 1985. Ichthyoplankton of the Flower Garden Banks, northwest Gulf of Mexico. Ph.D. Dissertation. University of Miami, Miami, Florida.

Meekan, M.G., M.J. Milicich, and P.J. Doherty. 1993. Larval production drives temporal patterns of larval supply and recruitment of a coral reef damselfish. Marine Ecology Progress Series 93: 217-225.

McClure, M.R. and J.D. McEachern. 1992. Hybridization between *Prionotus alatus* and *Prionotus paralatus* in the northern Gulf of Mexico. Copeia 4: 1039-46.

Parker, R.H. 1960. Ecology and distributional pattern of marine invertebrates, northern Gulf of Mexico. In: Shepard, F.P., F.B. Phleger and T.H. van Andel, eds. Recent Sediments, Northwest Gulf of Mexico. American Association of Petroleum Geologists.

Patillo, M.E., T.E. Czapla, D.M. Nelson, and M.E. Monaco. 1997. Distribution and abundance of fishes and invertebrates in Gulf of Mexico estuaries, Volume II: Species life history summaries. ELMR Report Number 11, NOAA/NOS Strategic Environmental Assessments Division, Silver Spring.

Pickering, H. and D. Whitmarsh. 1997. Artificial reefs and fisheries exploitation: a review of the 'attraction versus production' debate, the influence of design and its significance for policy. Fisheries Research 31: 39-59.

Pitcher, C.R. 1988. Spatial variation in the temporal pattern of recruitment of a coral reef damselfish. Proceedings of the International Coral Reef Symposium, 6th 2: 811-816.

Richards, W.J. 1984. Kinds and abundances of fish larvae in the Caribbean Sea and adjacent areas. NOAA Technical Report NMFS SSRF-776.

Richards, W.J., M.F. McGowan, T. Leming, J.T. Lamkin, and S. Kelley. 1993. Larval fish assemblages at the Loop Current boundary in the Gulf of Mexico. Bulletin of Marine Science 53(2): 475-537.

Robertson, D.R. 1991. The role of adult biology in the timing of spawning of tropical reef fishes. In: Sale, P.F., ed. The Ecology of Fishes on Coral Reefs. San Diego: Academic Press.

Robertson, D.R., D.G. Green, and B.C. Victor. 1988. Temporal coupling of production and recruitment of larvae of a Caribbean reef fish. Ecology 69: 370-381.

Robins, C.R., G.C. Ray, and J. Douglass. 1986. A Field Guide to the Atlantic Coast Fishes of North America. Houghton Mifflin Company, Boston, MA. 354 pp.

Robins, C.R., R.M. Bailey, C.E. Bond, J.R. Brooker, E.A. Lachner, R.N. Lea, and W.B. Scott. 1991. Common and scientific names of fishes from the United States and Canada. American Fisheries Society Special Publication 20. American Fisheries Society, Bethesda, MD.

Rooker, J.R., G. D. Dennis, and D. Goulet. 1996. Sampling larval fishes with a nightlight lift-net in tropical inshore waters. Fisheries Research 26: 1-15.

Rooker, J.R., Q.R. Dokken, C.V. Pattengill, and G.J. Holt. 1997. Fish assemblages on artificial and natural reefs in the Flower Garden Banks National Marine Sanctuary. Coral Reefs 16: 83-92.

Sabatés, A. and M. Pilar Olivar. 1996. Variation of larval fish distributions associated with variability in the location of a shelf-slope front. Marine Ecology Progress Series 135: 11-20.

Sale, P.F. 1980. The ecology of fishes on coral reefs. Oceanography and Marine Biology 18: 367-421.

SAS Institute, Inc. 1989. SAS/STAT Users Guide, Version 6. Cary: SAS Institute, Inc.

Scarborough-Bull, A. and J.J. Kendall, Jr. 1994. An indication of the process: offshore platforms as artificial reefs in the Gulf of Mexico. Bulletin of Marine Science 55: 1086-1098.

SEAMAP (Southeast Area Monitoring and Assessment Program). 2000. Environmental and biological atlas of the Gulf of Mexico 1998. Number 75. Gulf States Marine Fisheries Commission, Ocean Springs.

Shipp, R.L. 1992. Biogeography of Alabama's marine fishes. In: Boschung, H.T., Jr., ed. Catalog of freshwater and marine fishes of Alabama. Alabama Museum of Natural History Number 14: 7-9.

Shulman, M.J. 1985. Recruitment of coral reef fishes: effects of distribution of predators and shelter. Ecology 66: 1056-1066.

Smith, G.B. 1976. Ecology and distribution of eastern Gulf of Mexico reef fishes. Florida Marine Research Publications 19. 78 pp.

Sonnier, F., J. Teerling and H.D. Hoese. 1976. Observation on the offshore reef and platform fish fauna of Louisiana. Copeia 1976: 105-111.

Sponaugle, S. and R.K. Cowen. 1994. Larval durations and recruitment patterns of two Caribbean gobies (Gobiidae): contrasting early life histories in demersal spawners. Marine Biology 120: 133-143.

SPSS, Inc. 1999. SYSTAT 9: Getting started. Chicago: SPSS, Inc.

Stanley, D.R. and C.A. Wilson. 2000. Seasonal and spatial variation in the biomass and size frequency distribution of fish associated with oil and gas platforms in the northern Gulf of Mexico. OCS Study MMS 2000-005. U.S. Department of the Interior, Minerals Management Service, Gulf of Mexico OCS Region, New Orleans.

Sweatman, H.P.A. 1988. Field evidence that settling coral reef fish larvae detect resident fishes using dissolved chemical cues. Journal of Experimental Marine Biology and Ecology 124: 163-174.

Szedlmayer, S.T. and J. Conti. 1998. Nursery habitats, growth rates, and seasonality of age-0 red snapper, *Lutjanus campechanus*, in the northeast Gulf of Mexico. Fishery Bulletin 97: 626-635.

Thorrold, S.R. and D. McB. Williams. 1996. Meso-scale distribution patterns of larval and pelagic juvenile fishes in the central Great Barrier Reef Lagoon. Marine Ecology Progress Series. 145: 17-31.

Tolan, J.M. 2001. Patterns of reef fish larval supply to petroleum platforms in the northern Gulf of Mexico. Ph.D. dissertation. Louisiana State University, Baton Rouge.

Ursin, R. 1982. Stability and variability in the marine ecosystem. Dana Report 2: 51-67.

Victor, B.C. 1983. Recruitment and population dynamics of a coral reef fish. Science 219: 419-420.

Victor, B.C. 1986. Larval settlement and juvenile mortality in a recruitment-limited coral reef fish population. Ecological Monographs 56: 145-160.

Victor, B.C. 1987. Growth, dispersal, and identification of planktonic labrid and pomacentrid reef-fish larvae in the eastern Pacific Ocean. Marine Biology 95: 145-152.

Watson, W. 1996a. Blenniidae: combtooth blennies. In: H.G. Moser, ed. The early life history stages of fishes in the California Current region. CalCOFI Atlas No. 33. Lawrence, Kansas: Allen Press, Inc.

Watson, W. 1996b. Pomacentridae: damselfishes. In: H.G. Moser, ed. The early life history stages of fishes in the California Current region. CalCOFI Atlas No. 33. Lawrence, Kansas: Allen Press, Inc.

Watson, W. 2000. Blenniidae. In: J.M. Leis and B.M. Carson-Ewart (eds). The larvae of Indo-Pacific coastal fishes: an identification guide to marine fish larvae. Fauna Malesiana Handbooks. Boston, MA: Brill Publishing. 850 pp.

Williams, D. McB. 1983. Daily, monthly, and yearly variability in recruitment of a guild of coral reef fishes. Marine Ecology Progress Series 10: 231-237.

Zar, J.H. 1984. Biostatistical Analysis. Englewood Cliffs, New Jersey: Prentice Hall. 718 pp.

The Department of the Interior Mission

As the Nation's principal conservation agency, the Department of the Interior has responsibility for most of our nationally owned public lands and natural resources. This includes fostering sound use of our land and water resources; protecting our fish, wildlife, and biological diversity; preserving the environmental and cultural values of our national parks and historical places; and providing for the enjoyment of life through outdoor recreation. The Department assesses our energy and mineral resources and works to ensure that their development is in the best interests of all our people by encouraging stewardship and citizen participation in their care. The Department also has a major responsibility for American Indian reservation communities and for people who live in island territories under U.S. administration.

The Minerals Management Service Mission

As a bureau of the Department of the Interior, the Minerals Management Service's (MMS) primary responsibilities are to manage the mineral resources located on the Nation's Outer Continental Shelf (OCS), collect revenue from the Federal OCS and onshore Federal and Indian lands, and distribute those revenues.

Moreover, in working to meet its responsibilities, the **Offshore Minerals Management Program** administers the OCS competitive leasing program and oversees the safe and environmentally sound exploration and production of our Nation's offshore natural gas, oil and other mineral resources. The MMS **Minerals Revenue Management** meets its responsibilities by ensuring the efficient, timely and accurate collection and disbursement of revenue from mineral leasing and production due to Indian tribes and allottees, States and the U.S. Treasury.

The MMS strives to fulfill its responsibilities through the general guiding principles of: (1) being responsive to the public's concerns and interests by maintaining a dialogue with all potentially affected parties and (2) carrying out its programs with an emphasis on working to enhance the quality of life for all Americans by lending MMS assistance and expertise to economic development and environmental protection.